HOUSES EXTENSIONS. Creating new open spaces

Editor, concept, and project director
Anna Minguet

Art director and project's selection
Eva Minguet (Monsa Publications)
Layout
Patricia Martínez (Monsa Publications)
Cover design
Eva Minguet, Patricia Martínez (Monsa Publications)
Text edition
Monsa Publications

INSTITUTO MONSA DE EDICIONES
Gravina 43 (08930)
Sant Adrià de Besòs
Barcelona (Spain)
Tlf. +34 93 381 00 50
www.monsa.com
monsa@monsa.com

Cover image © Martin Gardner (Austen House Pod)

ISBN: 978-84-16500-47-5
D.L. B 6691-2017
Printed by Cachimán Grafic

HOUSES EXTENSIONS

creating new open spaces

monsa

INTRO

When much of our existing housing stock was built, lifestyles were very different. This has meant that a large proportion of architect's work has been adapting these older buildings, rather than building afresh. We have needed to develop new skills. The challenge is thus to adapt our old buildings to our new ways of living, whilst not destroying what we like about the older houses.

Adaption will often mean adding more space. This will often be to the back, the roof or the side, or even sometimes underneath, whilst retaining the original building's front as part of the streetscape. But it can also mean radical changes to the way the interiors are organized. Most older buildings are very cellular, reflecting the available building technology and social conventions at the time. But we like to live in much more open and airy spaces, and new structural materials and building methods make it straightforward to remove walls and free the space.

Modern designers have a whole new world of materials and technologies at hand to build our new homes. Glass technology has transformed what we can do with daylight. Its thermal performance has improved so much that we can enjoy large expanses, connecting inside and outside, without heat gain or loss. The introduction of the steel frame into domestic architecture has meant it is easy to make large open spaces. This open plan has been embraced as the preferred family space, with room for cooking, dining and socializing, all in the same area.

This book is about the challenge of adapting our old buildings to our new lifestyles in lots of different and creative ways. Old buildings have proved themselves flexible to changing necessities, and are key to the regeneration of our built environment.

Cuando la mayor parte de las viviendas existentes se construyeron, el estilo de vida de las familias que las habitaban era muy distinto. Una parte muy importante del trabajo arquitectónico ha sido adaptar estos edificios a los nuevos tiempos para no construirlos de nuevo. Y este tipo de trabajo ha implicado el desarrollo de nuevas habilidades. El reto es por ello adaptar nuestros antiguos edificios a nuestra forma moderna de vivir, sin destruir lo que apreciamos de estas viviendas.

Y la adaptación ha significado, en muchas ocasiones, añadir más espacio. Muchas veces en la parte de atrás, en un lateral o en el tejado, e incluso por debajo, para mantener intacta la fachada principal del edificio como parte del paisaje urbanístico. Pero también puede implicar un cambio radical en la forma de organizar el interior de la vivienda. La mayoría de los edificios antiguos están muy compartimentados, reflejando la tecnología de construcción disponible en su época y las convenciones sociales del momento. Pero hoy en día preferimos vivir en espacios abiertos y amplios. Gracias a los nuevos materiales estructurales y los métodos de construcción actuales se pueden eliminar paredes y liberar el espacio.

Los diseñadores modernos tienen a su alcance un nuevo mundo de materiales y tecnologías para la construcción de nuevos hogares. La tecnología del vidrio ha transformado lo que podemos hacer con la luz natural. Su eficiencia térmica ha mejorado tanto que podemos disfrutar de grandes superficies de cristal que conectan interior y exterior sin perder o ganar calor. La introducción de los perfiles de acero en la arquitectura residencial ha facilitado conseguir grandes espacios abiertos. Esta zona abierta se ha convertido en el espacio preferido de la familia: un lugar para cocinar, comer y socializar, todo en el mismo lugar.

Este libro trata el reto de adaptar nuestros antiguos edificios a nuestra nueva forma de vida, de muchas formas distintas y muy creativas. Los edificios originales se han mostrado flexibles al cambio de necesidades y claves para la regeneración de nuestro entorno.

Text by Paul Archer (architect director at Paul Archer Design)

EXTENSION VUGHT

Transformation of a low and dark basement

Burokoek

VUGHT, THE NETHERLANDS

Photos © StijnStijl

Total Building Area: 775 sq ft – 72 m²
Extension Area: 215 sq ft – 20 m² // 28% of total area

This extending renovation of an existing townhouse was necessary to satisfy the needs of a large family. With an upper ground floor above street level and a garden at the rear of the property sunken at basement level, the house suffered from a lack of easy access between the living areas and the exterior. Whilst the basement had a low ceiling—and for this reason it was only used for storage—, it offered the opportunity and the potential for the creation of a spacious living area with direct access to the garden. By doing this, the ground floor would lend itself for a reorganization to accommodate other spatial needs of the family.

La gran familia que habitaba esta casa adosada necesitaba una ampliación de la misma. El desnivel del terreno –la planta baja está al nivel de la calle, mientras que el sótano se encuentra al nivel del jardín trasero– impedía una conexión directa entre la zona de vida y el exterior. Por su baja altura, el sótano solo se usaba para almacenaje. Sin embargo, tenía potencial para transformarse en una zona común espaciosa con acceso directo al jardín. Con este cambio, la planta baja se reorganizaría para albergar otras zonas necesarias para la familia.

The excavation of the basement to increase its ceiling height made possible to move the kitchen, living room and dining room—originally on the ground floor—down to the garden level. The existing garden staircase was internalized in a new window frame.

La excavación del sótano para incrementar la altura del techo hizo posible trasladar la cocina, la sala de estar y el comedor –originalmente en la planta baja– al nivel del jardín. La escalera existente del jardín se incluyó en la ampliación de cristal.

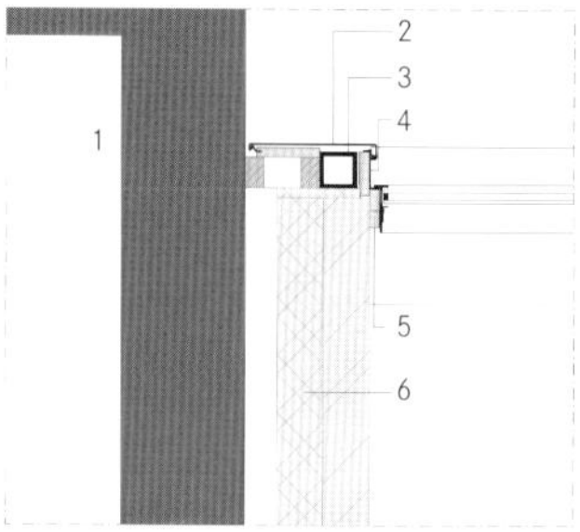

Detail 1

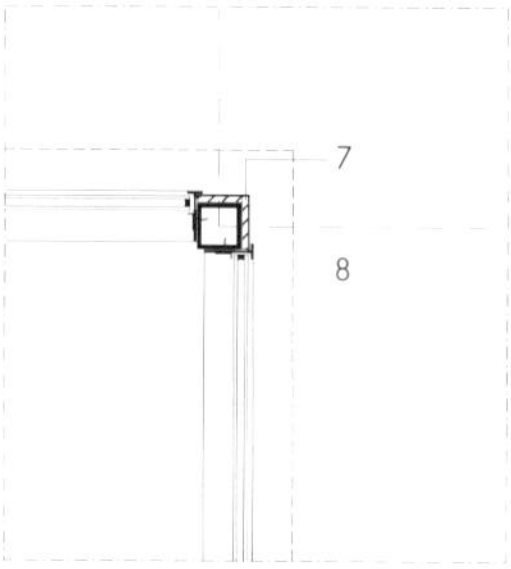

Detail 2

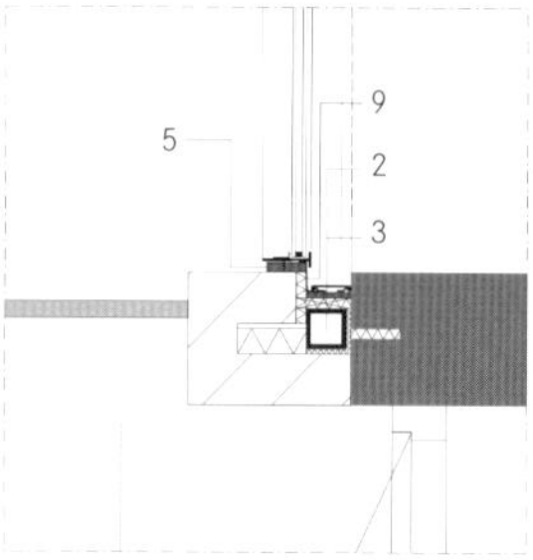

Detail 3

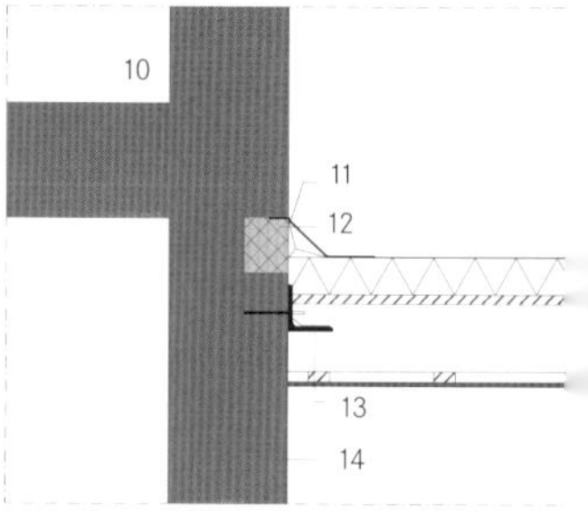

Detail 4

1. Adjacent property
2. Clip mounting zinc metal sheet
3. 80 x 80 tube
4. Black zinc
5. 20 mm wood block
6. 100 mm insulation
7. 12 mm plywood + Sendzimir sheet
8. Steel column 90 x 90 x 6 mm
9. 1.5 mm Sendzimir sheet
10. Existing floor slab
11. Metal flashing
12. Cellular concrete (thermal bridge break)
13. 100 x 100 x 10 mm steel angle
14. Exposed original masonry wall

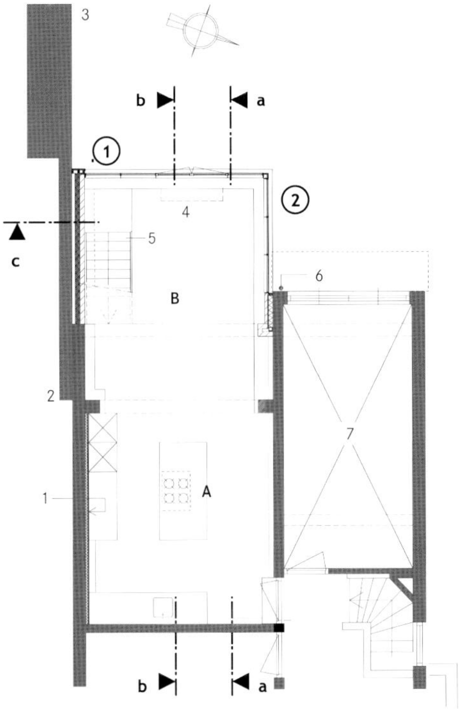

New half basement floor plan

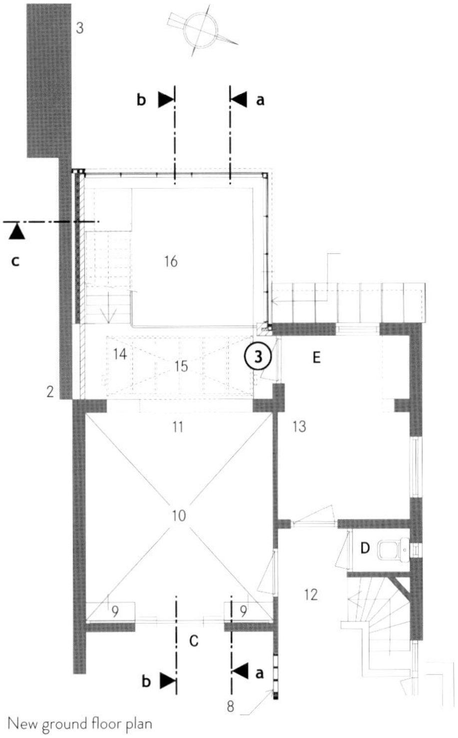

New ground floor plan

- A. Kitchen
- B. Dining area
- C. Living area
- D. WC room
- E. Office

1. New double wall to mitigate moisture problem through existing exterior wall
2. Adjacent party wall
3. Adjacent building
4. New oak step
5. Existing steel staircase with new oak treads
6. Downspout
7. Room remains unchanged
8. Doorway between living room and hallway sealed with plasterboard and stucco finish
9. Cabinet
10. Living room remains unchanged
11. Opening frame removed. Lintel remains. New stone threshold
12. Hall remains unchanged
13. Ceiling is maintained. Wall tiles are removed. Walls are plastered smooth
14. Existing landing remains unchanged
15. Skylight above
16. Open to below
17. Existing wall
18. Existing balcony
19. 46 x 146 beams
20. To existing sewer line
    46 x 146 beams + 18 mm
    plywood decking

sk1 = Steel column 90 x 90 x 6
sb1 = HE120A steel beam + steel column
sb2 = HE140A steel beam
sb3 = 100 x 100 x 10 steel angle

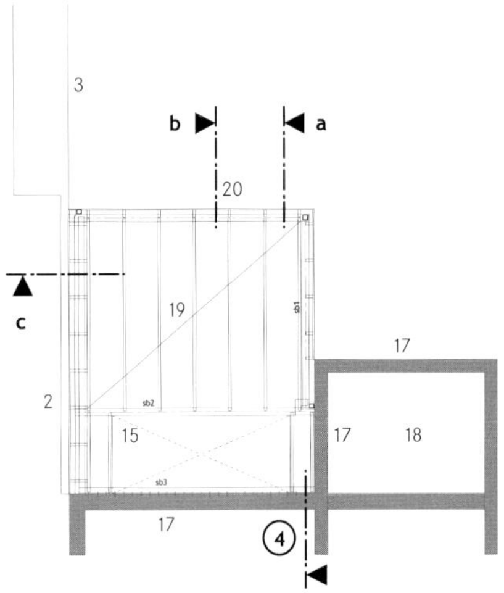

Framing plan

Computer generated rendering. Exterior view of extension.
Representación generada por ordenador. Vista exterior de la extensión.

Computer generated rendering. Interior view of extension.
Representación generada por ordenador. Vista interior de la extensión.

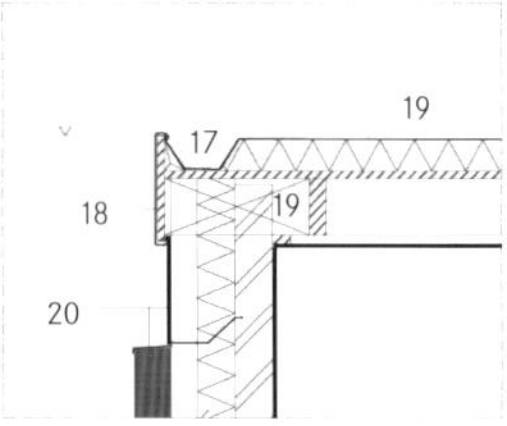

Detail 1

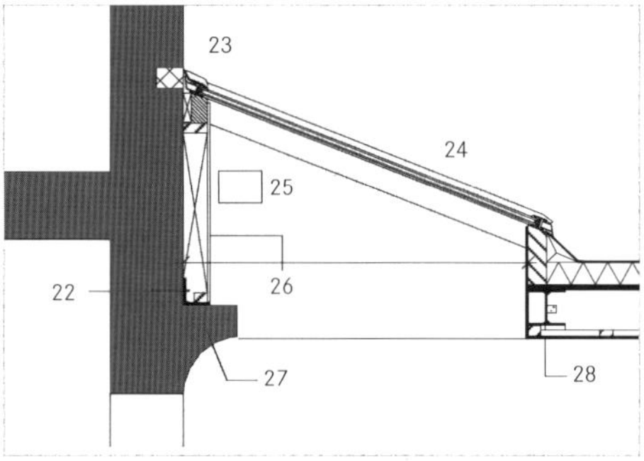

Detail 2

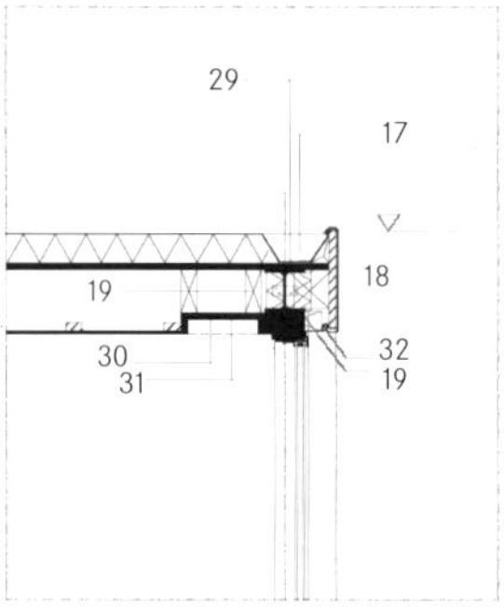

Detail 3

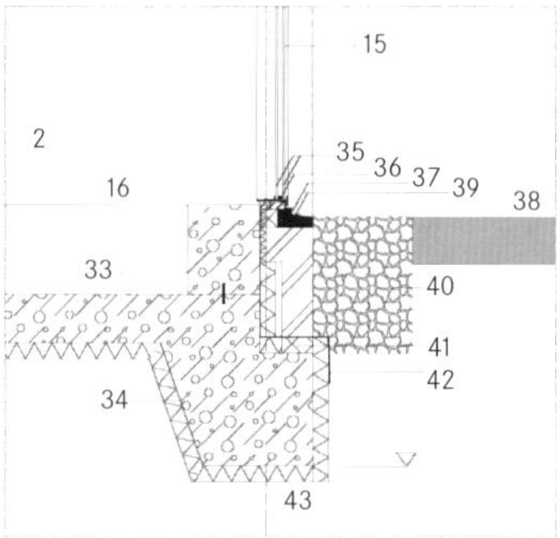

Detail 4

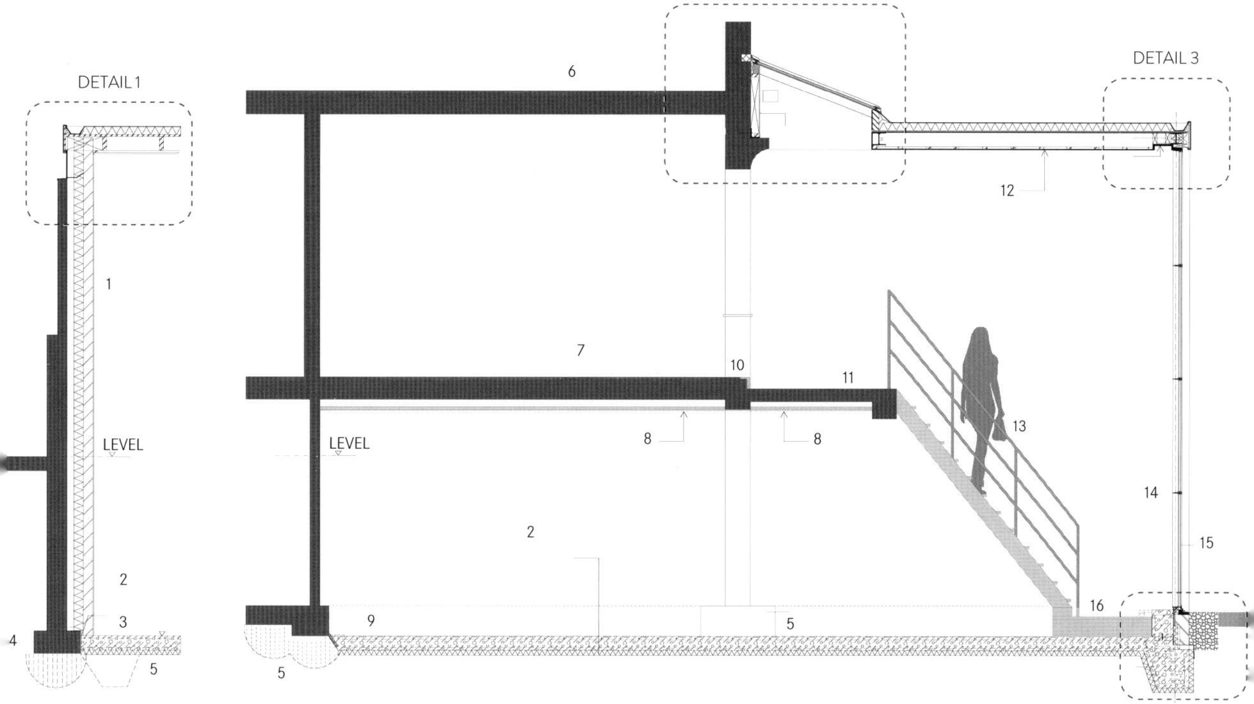

Section C

Section AA

1. Partition wall
   - Existing party wall
   - Limestone
   - 50 mm insulation
   - Brick wall (used brick)
2. Half basement floor
   - 150 mm concrete slab (with radiant heat)
   - 75 mm Floormate 500 insulation board
   - PE waterproofing membrane
   - Compacted sand bed
3. Thermal bridge break
4. Foundation depth of existing party wall unknown
5. Existing foundation to remain untouched
6. Second floor
   Existing floor and lintels unchanged
7. Ground floor
   Existing floor and lintels unchanged
8. Plasterboard ceiling, smooth plaster finish
9. New foundation connected to existing with chemical anchors
10. New hardwood threshold
11. Existing landing and lintels unchanged
12. Acoustic ceiling, smooth finish
13. Steel staircase with new oak treads
14. Door opening height 2300 mm min.
15. Window details by manufacturer
16. Wooden platform
17. Rain gutter
18. 20 mm plywood fascia + zinc sheet
19. Wood blocking
20. Stucco reveal and metal flashing
21. Flat roof detail
   - Bituminous roofing membrane
   - 80 mm min. rigid foam insulation
   - 18 mm plywood roof decking
   - 46 x 146 mm beam
   - 20 mm battens
   - Acoustic ceiling
22. 100 x 100 x 10 steel angle anchored to wall
23. Lead and cellular concrete
   (thermal bridge break)
24. Prefabricated skylight and support beams, painted white
25. Ventilation grill
26. Plasterboard
   45 x 90 furring
   10 mm plaster and stucco
27. Existing concrete lintel
28. HE140A beam
29. HE120A beam
30. 18 mm plywood
31. 50 x 200 ceiling cove
32. Black zinc
33. Rebar dia. 6-300
34. Rebar dia. 8-300
35. Safety glass
36. 20 mm plywood
37. Metal profile
38. Ground
39. Stone threshold
40. Gravel bed to prevent splashing
41. Cellular concrete
   (thermal bridge break)
42. Metal flashing
43. Floormate 500

In this living room-style kitchen, old and new come together symbiotically by, among other things, juxtaposing the old exposed bricks with the new concrete flooring, white oak woodwork, and steel railings and window frames.

En este salón con cocina abierta, lo antiguo y lo nuevo se unen y contrastan: los antiguos ladrillos vistos con el suelo nuevo de cemento; los remates de madera de roble blanca con las barandillas de acero y los marcos de las ventanas.

URBAN BEAT

Renovation and extension of a townhouse

WY-TO architects

MONTREUIL-SOUS-BOIS, FRANCE

Photos © Svend Andersen

Total Building Area: 1141 sq ft – 106 m^2
Extension Area: 431 sq ft – 40 m^2 // 38% of total area

The main purpose of this project was to extend the area of the family home. The client had inherited the house from her grandfather. Rather than having the house tore down, she decided to work with what she had inherited. The process of adding a new floor to an existing structure is far more complex than starting from scratch. It is, however, a tool for urban densification, whilst maintaining a reference to the past. It was decided that the vertical extension was going to be a wooden structure for its lightweight quality, its fast assembly, and clean construction. It appeared to be the ideal response to the existing dense context. This method of construction allowed the owner of the house to remain in it during the duration of construction.

El objetivo principal de este proyecto era ampliar el espacio de la vivienda familiar. Al recibir como herencia de su abuelo esta casa, el cliente decidió emprender su reforma en lugar de derruirla. Hay que tener en cuenta que el proceso de añadir una planta nueva a una estructura existente es mucho más complicado que empezar desde cero. Sin embargo, es una herramienta para la creciente densificación urbana que permite mantener al mismo tiempo las referencias al pasado. Se decidió que la extensión vertical sería una estructura de madera, por su ligereza, su facilidad de ensamblaje y su construcción limpia. Parecía la respuesta ideal a la densidad del contexto existente. Este método de construcción permitió que la dueña permaneciese en la vivienda durante la construcción.

LIVRETS D'OPERA
LIVRETS D'OPERA
TIM BURTON
RENOIR
Art & Sole
HUNTER S. THOMPSON
Marc Levy

Rather than blending the extension with the existing white-rendered walls, the architects created two distinct volumes clad in different woods: poplar and pine. The result is a simple, yet expressive composition, which reflects the character of the area's architecture.

En lugar de unir la extensión con las paredes existentes recubiertas en blanco, los arquitectos crearon dos volúmenes distintos revestidos de dos maderas diferentes: chopo y pino. El resultado es una composición sencilla pero muy expresiva, que refleja el carácter de la arquitectura de la zona.

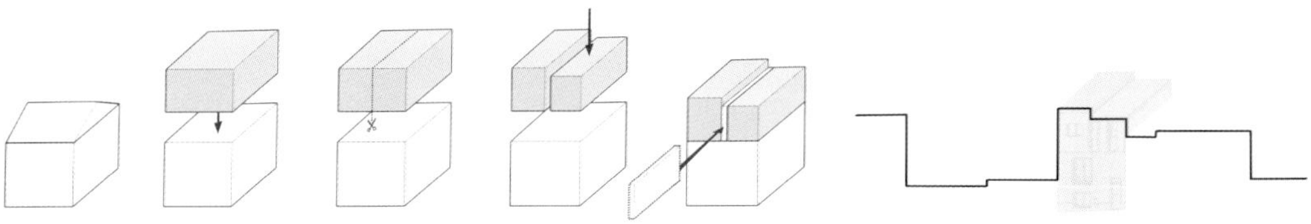

Conceptual design diagram

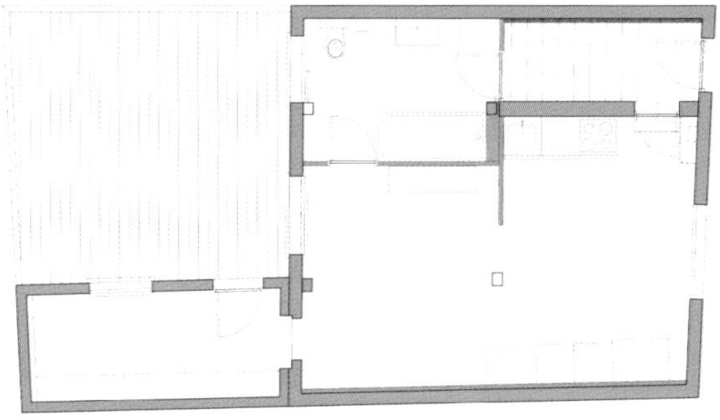

New floor plan

Original street elevation

New street elevation

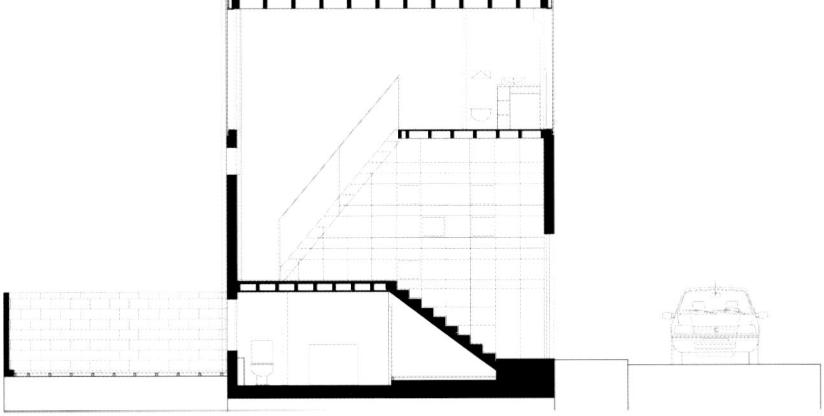

New building section

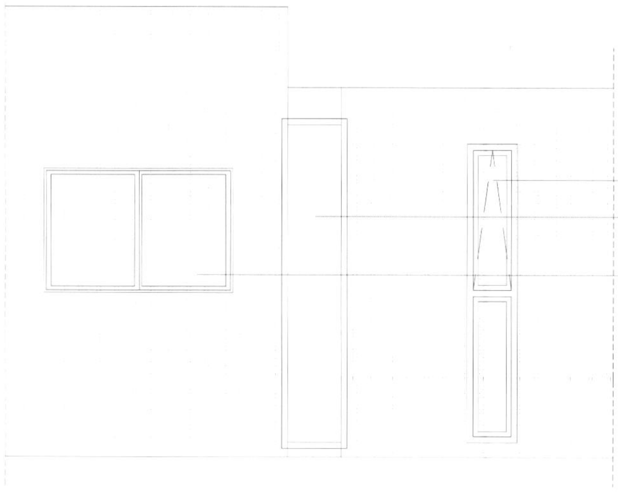

Partial wall elevation at extension

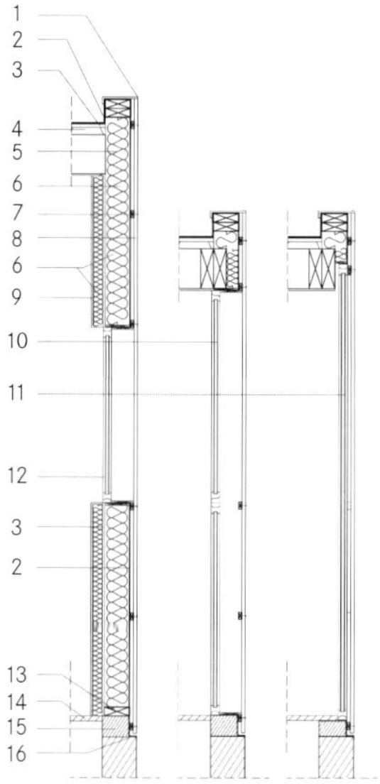

Section detail 1 Section detail 2 Section detail 3

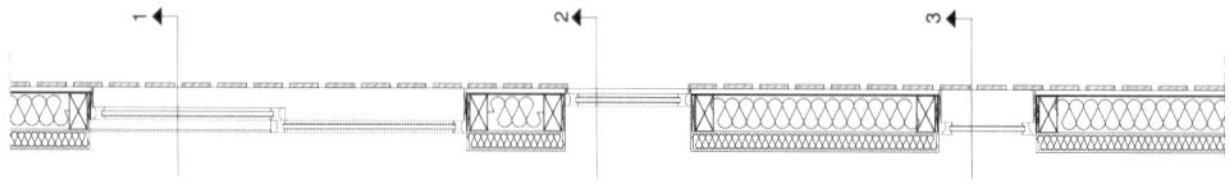

Partial plan detail at extension

1. Wall cap
2. Waterproof membrane
3. OSB shear wall panel
4. Metal decking
5. Top runner
6. Glass wool insulation
7. Furring strip
8. Wood siding
9. Facing material
10. Oscillating frame
11. Fixed frame
12. Sliding frame
13. Bottom runner
14. Flooring
15. Masonry base
16. Zinc flashing

The contemporary language of the exterior treatment of the addition permeates into the interior, where light and clean lines predominate.

El lenguaje contemporáneo del exterior penetra en el interior, donde siguen predominando la luz y las líneas puras.

CLIFFS IMPASSE

Beyond the walls

Ziegler Antonin architecte

SENNEVILLE-SUR-FÉCAMP, FRANCE

Photos © Antonin Ziegler

Total Building Area: 1184 sq ft – 110 m²
Extension Area: 646 sq ft – 60 m² // 54.5% of total area

The extension of an old rural stone house explores the idea of inserting new buildings into a landscape and their compatibility with existing structures. A glazed entry hall eases the transition between the house and a contemporary wooden extension, consisting of a black plywood box with no formal association with the existing building. The extension provides space for a garage on the ground floor and a reading room on the upper floor. Inserted into the existing house, a small staircase leads to a space high above the ground, which provides an escape from every known frame of reference, and offers an environment that promotes reflection and creativity.

El anexo de una antigua casa rural explora la idea de insertar nuevos edificios en un paisaje y su compatibilidad con estructuras existentes. Una entrada acristalada facilita la transición entre la casa y el anexo de madera contemporáneo, que está formado por una caja de madera contrachapada negra sin asociación directa con el edificio existente. Esta ampliación proporciona el espacio para un garaje en la planta baja y una biblioteca en la planta superior. Desde la vivienda original, una pequeña escalera conduce a un espacio elevado que proporciona un escape a cualquier escala de referencia y ofrece un entorno que invita a la reflexión y a la creatividad.

For the occupants of this small country house, the space felt cramped within its massive stone walls. They also didn't feel isolated enough, something they longed to better enjoy their reading and writing.

Los habitantes de esta pequeña casa de campo sentían que el espacio se contraía dentro de sus grandes muros de piedra. Tampoco se sentían suficientemente aislados, algo que anhelaban para disfrutar completamente de la lectura y escritura.

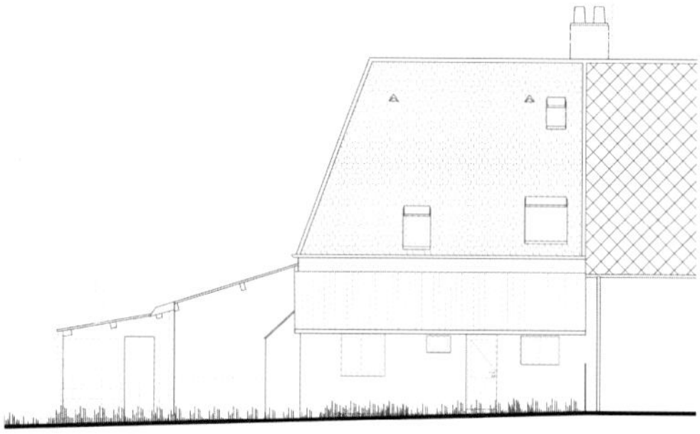

Original south-west building elevation

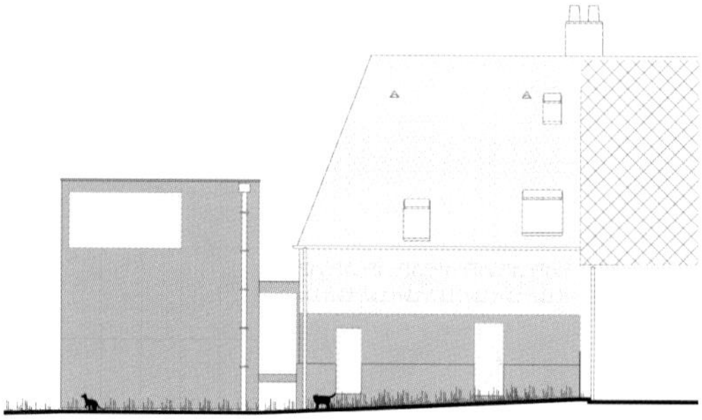

New south-west elevation

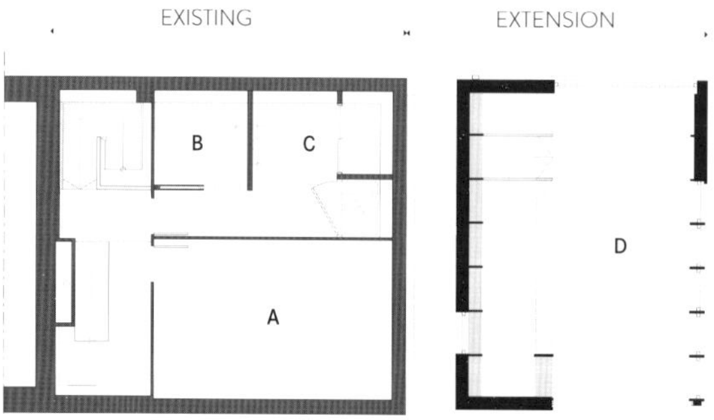

New second floor

A. Bedroom
B. Laundry room
C. Bathroom
D. Library

Original north-west building elevation

New north-west elevation

Original north-east building elevation

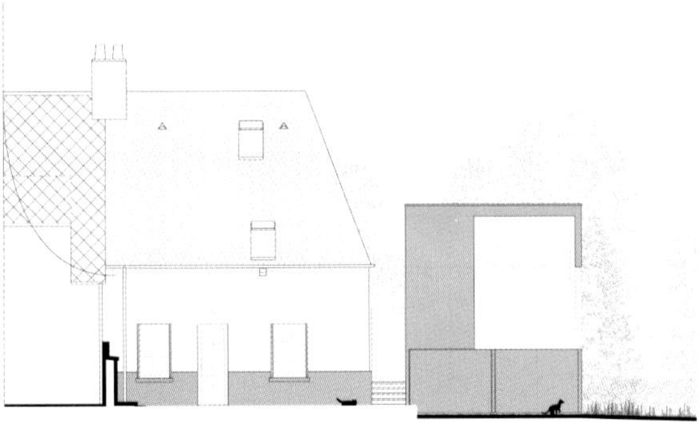

New north-east elevation

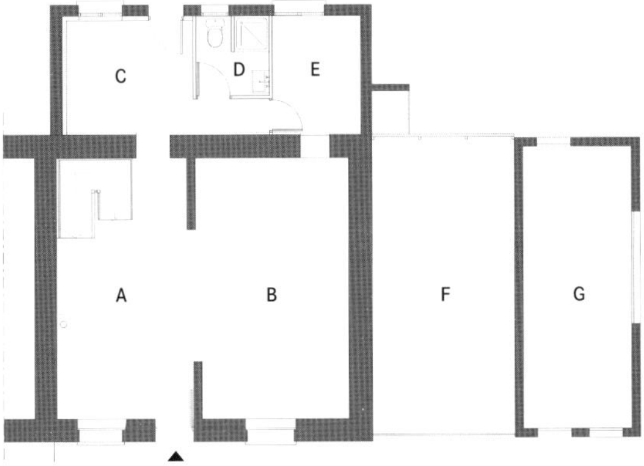

Original ground floor plan

A. Dining room
B. Living room
C. Kitchen
D. Bathroom
E. Laundry room
F. Garage
G. Storage room

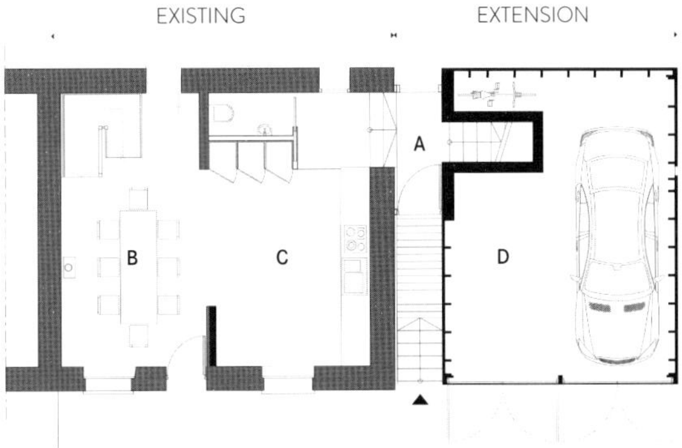

New ground floor plan

A. Entrance
B. Dining room
C. Kitchen
D. Garage

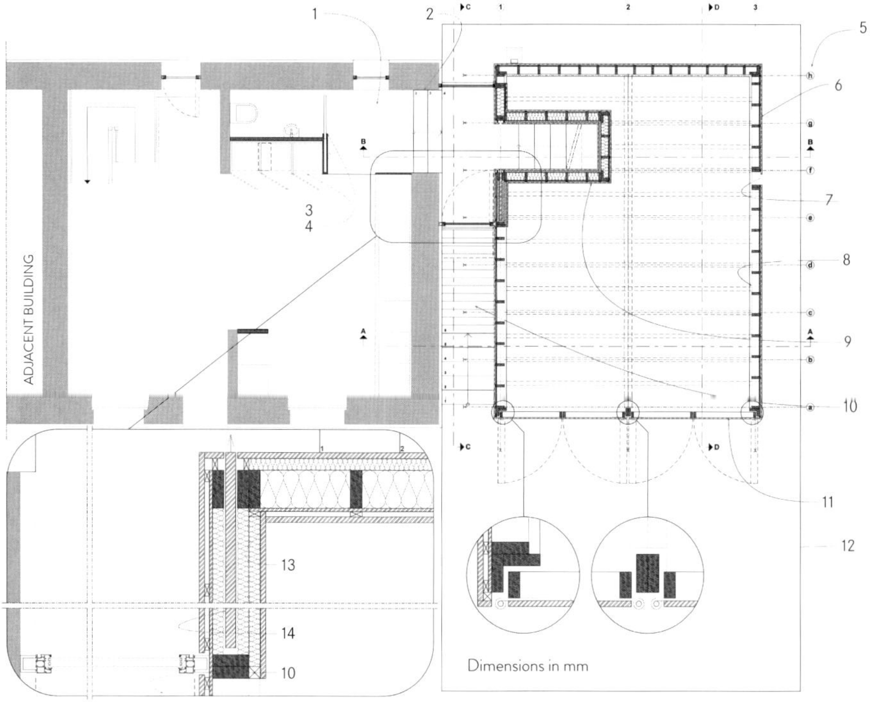

Ground floor plan framing details

1. Subfloor
   - 12 mm okoume plywood flooring
   - Clear wood stain
2. Door framing in the continuity of existing walls and ceilings
3. Kitchen equipment to be determined
4. Plasterboard + pocket door
5. Structural floor framing, 90`cm on centre
6. - 22 mm thick exterior grade okoume plywood panels
   - Black pine tar protection layer
   - 20 x 45 mm battens
   - Waterproof membrane
   - 12 mm OSB
   - 45 x 145 mm uprights
7. Vertical opening through ground and second floor
8. Bituminous coating (black) on all wall faces (including tops)
9. Staircase wood frame
   - 12 mm okoume plywood flooring
   - Transparent wood stain
   - Sound insulation 30 mm
   - 18 mm OSB wall sheathing
   - Vapour barrier
   - 225 x 75 mm stringers
   - Insulation 200 mm
   - Support beam 25 x 50
   - 6 mm OSB subfloor
   - Riser = 19 cm
   - Tread = 31 cm
10. Wood decking (1 cm spaces between boards)
    - Non-slip wood slats
    - Lay of the slats perpendicular to existing wall
11. Double-leaf garage door
    - Finish to match exterior wall finish
    - Door face to be flush with face of building
12. Black basalt gravel over stabilizing drainage slab
13. - 22 mm thick interior grade okoume plywood panels
    - Black pine tar protection layer
    - 20 x 45 mm battens
    - Waterproof membrane
    - 12 mm OSB
    - 45 x 145 mm uprights
    - Insulation 150 mm
    - Pocket door
    - 45 x 45 mm uprights
    - Waterproof membrane
    - Exterior OSB panel
14. Pocket door
    - 22 mm thick exterior grade okoume plywood panels
    - Black pine tar protection layer
    - 22 mm thick interior okoume plywood panel
    - Clear wood stain

Exterior cladding – wall caps and other lacquered aluminium parts painted in RAL 9005 (unless otherwise noted)

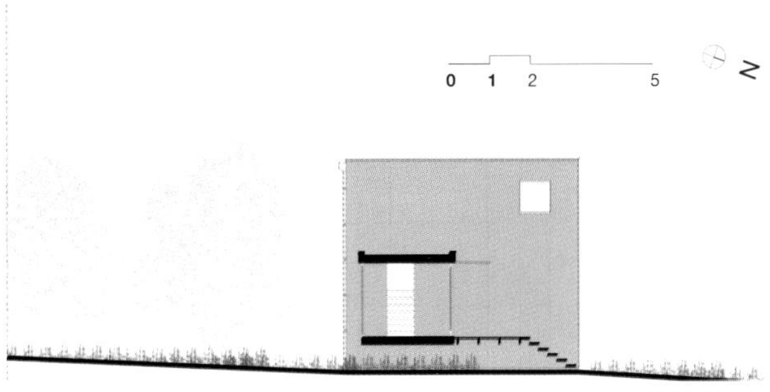

Section through entrance, facing extension

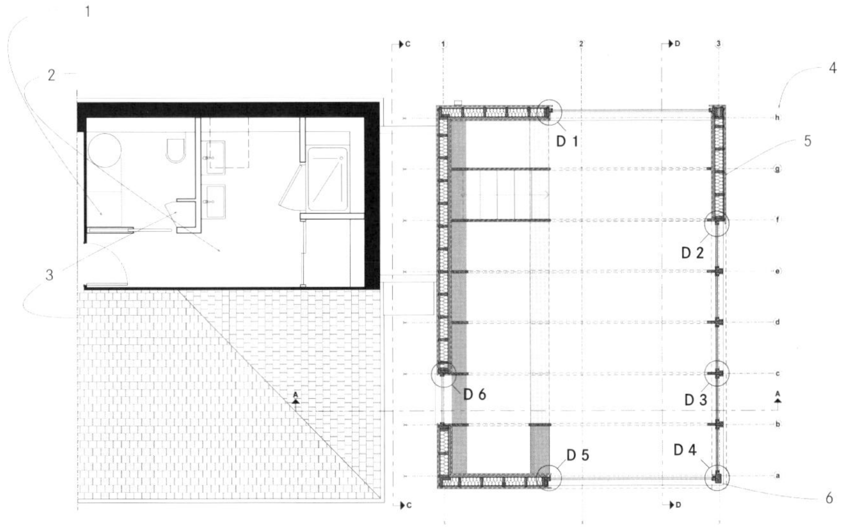

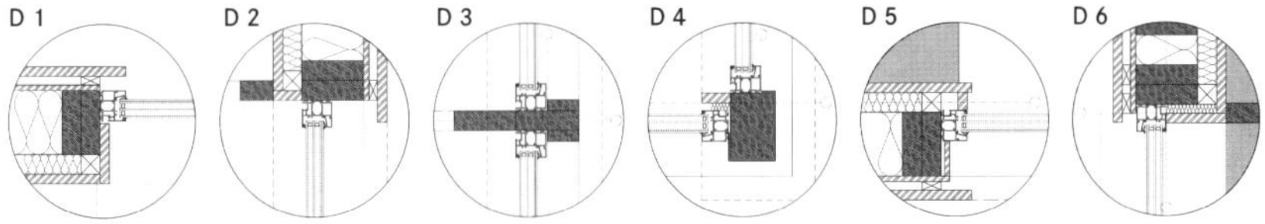

Second floor plan framing details

1. Mechanically controlled ventilation, single flow self-adjustment in isolated service duct (acoustic insulation) + access hatch
2. Fitting of a bathroom + laundry room on second floor
   - Partitioning + equipment + electricity
   - Flooring: to be varnished
   - Wall ceramic tile (over moisture-resistant plasterboard), full height in shower and at washbasins
3. Mechanically controlled ventilation, single flow self-adjustment (roof exit), and access hatch at highest point
   - Exposed ducts in rigid, flat and rectangular conduits
4. Structural floor framing, 90 cm on centre
5. - 22 mm thick exterior grade okoume plywood panels
   - Black pine tar protection layer
   - 20 x 45 mm battens
   - Waterproof membrane
   - 12 mm OSB
   - 45 x 145 mm uprights
6. Sheet metal, lacquered in RAL to match building finish over wood post

Exterior cladding – wall caps and other lacquered aluminium parts painted in RAL 9005 (unless otherwise noted)

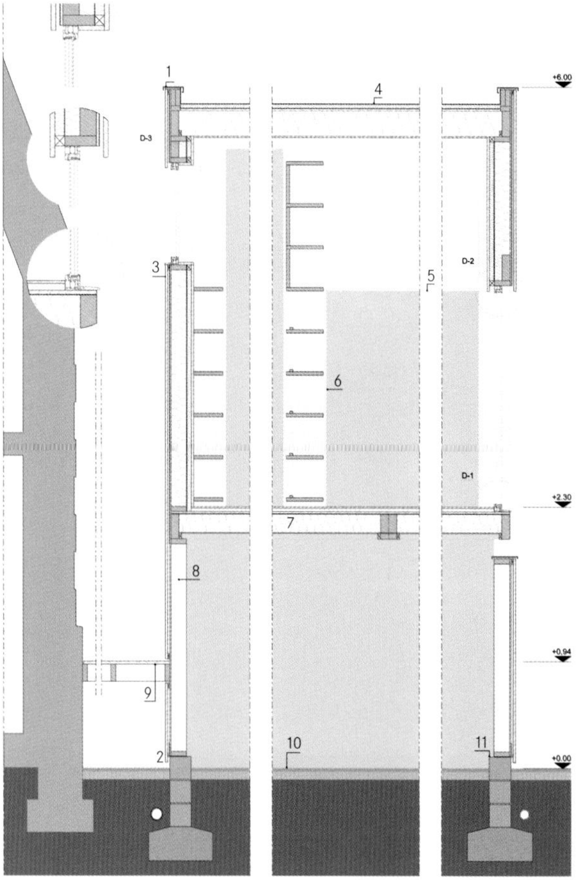

Exterior cladding – wall caps and other lacquered aluminium parts painted in RAL 9005 (unless otherwise noted)

Detail section AA

1. Lacquered wall cap, 30`mm max. on wall face
2. Lower part of the exterior wall at 50 mm above ground max. (constant height to be respected on all exterior wall)
3. - 22 mm thick exterior grade okoume plywood panels
   - Black pine tar protection layer
   - 20 x 45 mm battens
   - Waterproof membrane
   - 12 mm OSB
   - 45 x 145 mm uprights
   - Insulation 150 mm
   - Vapour barrier
   - 45 x 45 uprights
   - Insulation 50 mm
   - 22 mm thick interior okoume plywood panel
   - Clear wood stain
4. Wood framing of roof terrace
   - Waterproofing
   - 40 mm insulating panel
   - Vapour barrier
   - 21 mm OSB
   - 225 x 75 panels
   - 200 mm insulation
   - 22 mm thick interior okoume plywood panel
   - Clear wood stain
5. Alignment to be respected
6. Decorative wooden structure in planed spruce
   - Framing at 90 cm on centre
   - 45 x 400 mm sections (vertical elements) and 30 x 340 mm sections (horizontal sections)
7. Wood floor framing
   - 12 mm okoume plywood flooring
   - Clear wood stain
   - Sound insulation 30 mm
   - 18 mm OSB wall sheathing
   - Vapour barrier
   - 225 x 75 panels
   - 200 mm insulation
   - 25 x 50 support beam
   - 6 mm OSB subfloor
8. - 22 mm thick exterior grade okoume plywood panels
   - Black pine tar protection layer
   - 20 x 45 mm battens
   - Waterproof membrane
   - 12 mm OSB
   - 45 x 145 mm uprights
9. Wood decking (1 cm spaces between boards)
   - Non-slip wood slats
   - Lay of the slats perpendicular to existing wall
10. Black basalt gravel over stabilizing drainage slab
11. Bituminous coating (black) on all wall faces (including tops)

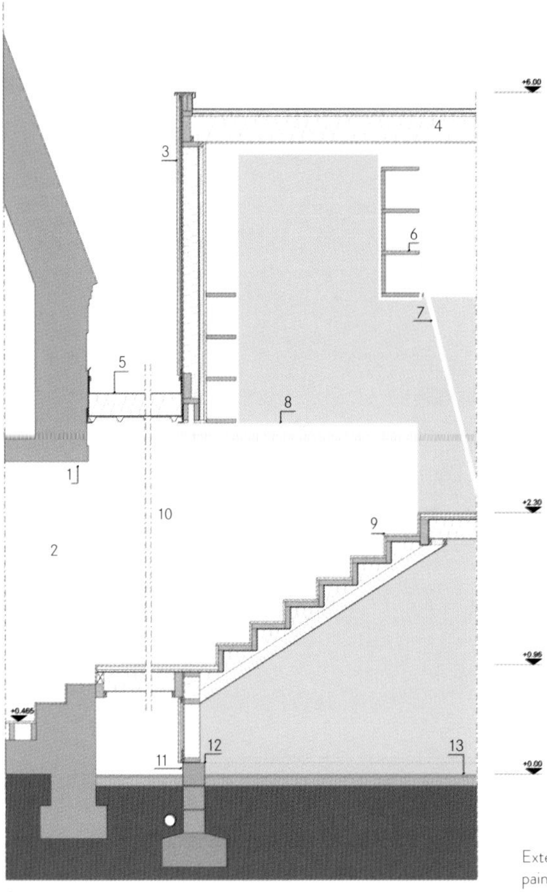

Exterior cladding – wall caps and other lacquered aluminium parts painted in RAL 9005 (unless otherwise noted)

Detail section BB

1. Door framing in the continuity of existing walls and ceilings
2. - Subfloor
   - 12 mm okoume plywood flooring
   - Clear wood stain
3. - 22 mm thick exterior grade okoume plywood panels
   - Black pine tar protection layer
   - 20 x 45 mm battens
   - Waterproof membrane
   - 12 mm OSB
   - 45 x 145 mm uprights
   - Insulation 150 mm
   - Vapour barrier
   - 45 x 45 uprights
   - Insulation 50 mm
   - 22 mm thick interior okoume plywood panel
   - Clear wood stain
4. Wood framing of roof terrace
   - Waterproofing
   - 40 mm insulating panel
   - Vapour barrier
   - 21 mm OSB
   - 225 x 75 panels
   - 200 mm insulation
   - 22 mm thick interior okoume plywood panel
   - Clear wood stain
5. Waterproof steel roof
   - Waterproofing
   - 200 mm insulation
   - Vapour barrier
   - Lacquered corrugated metal sheet
6. - Decorative wooden structure in planed spruce
   - Framing at 90 cm on centre
   - 45 x 400 mm sections (vertical elements) and 30 x 340 mm sections (horizontal sections)
7. Library sliding ladder
8. Alignment to be respected (guardrail/shelf/lintel)
9. Staircase wood frame
   - 12 mm okoume plywood flooring
   - Transparent wood stain
   - Sound insulation 30 mm
   - 18 mm OSB wall sheathing
   - Vapour barrier
   - 225 x 75 mm stringers
   - Insulation 200 mm
   - Support beam 25 x 50
   - 6 mm OSB subfloor
   - Riser = 19 cm
   - Tread = 31 cm
10. Pocket door
    - 22 mm thick exterior grade okoume plywood panels
    - Black pine tar protection layer
    - 22 mm thick interior okoume plywood panel
    - Clear wood stain
11. Lower part of the exterior wall at 50 mm above ground max. (constant height to be respected on all exterior wall)
12. Bituminous coating (black) on all wall faces (including tops)
13. Black basalt gravel over stabilizing drainage slab

Open on three sides, the interior space is exposed to the views, like a book opened to the landscape. Its open character is complemented by the warmth bought by the wooden surfaces and the lighting.

Abierto por tres lados, el espacio interior se muestra a la vistas, como un libro expuesto al paisaje. Su carácter abierto se complementa con la calidez que aportan las superficies de madera y la iluminación.

Beyond offering views and providing a place for evasion, the space also creates a new relationship with the surrounding natural landscape in a way that the original house can't offer.

Además de ofrecer grandes vistas y un lugar para evadirse, el anexo también crea una nueva relacion con el paisaje que lo rodea, que la casa original no podía ofrecer.

FEISTEINVEIEN

Preserving the original house distinctive identity

Rever & Drage architects

STAVANGER, NORWAY

Photos © Tom Auger

Total Building Area: 1615 sq ft – 150 m²
Extension Area: 1356 sq ft – 126 m² // 84% of total area

This extension to an existing single-family home was intended to make room for a growing family in a city, which has become increasingly dense over the last decades due to the economic boom related to the area's oil industry. The building authorities accepted an extension beyond the original restrictions, but wanted a modern expression. The concept of the project defines a modular extension that helps redefine the functional program of the house without obscuring the original character of the existing building. Rather, it lets it take centre stage as the heart of the home.

La bonanza económica relacionada con la industria del petróleo de la zona ha originado un aumento de la densidad de población en la ciudad en las últimas décadas. Por ello, el objetivo de esta ampliación de una vivienda unifamiliar urbana existente era dar cabida a una familia en crecimiento. Las autoridades urbanísticas aceptaron una extensión más allá de las restricciones originales, pero querían una construcción moderna. El concepto del proyecto define una extensión modular que ayuda a redefinir el programa funcional de la casa sin ocultar el carácter original del edificio existente. Más bien, permite que el espacio central sea el corazón de la vivienda.

The authorities and the architects agreed in that the existing building would be preserved intact to honour the architectural heritage of the area. Extension and addition stand out from each other by contrasting colours.

Las autoridades y los arquitectos estuvieron de acuerdo en preservar el edificio existente por respeto a la herencia arquitectónica de la zona. La extensión y los añadidos destacan uno del otro debido al contraste de colores.

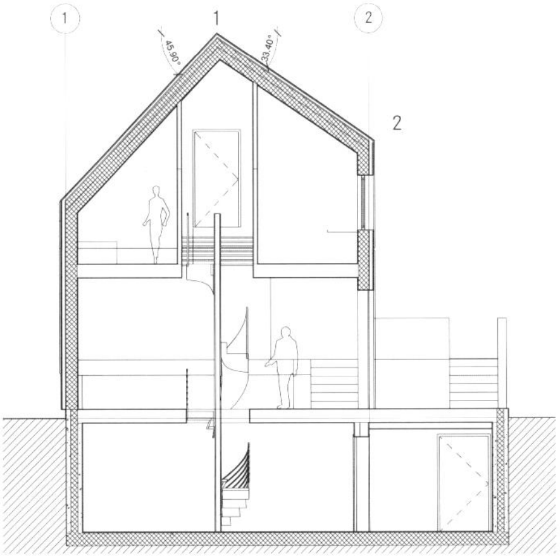

Section 1

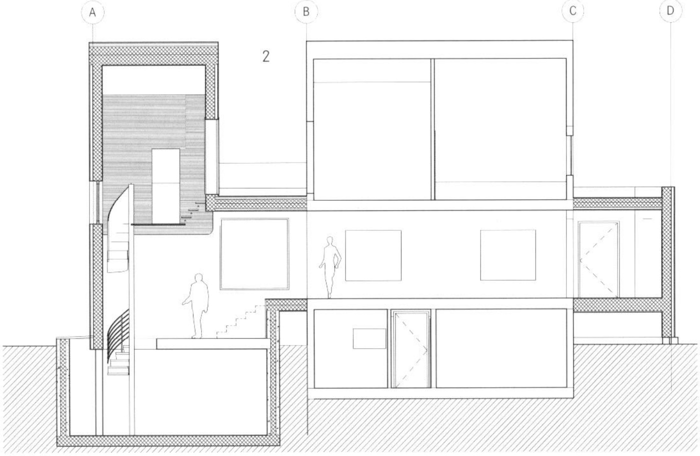

Section 2

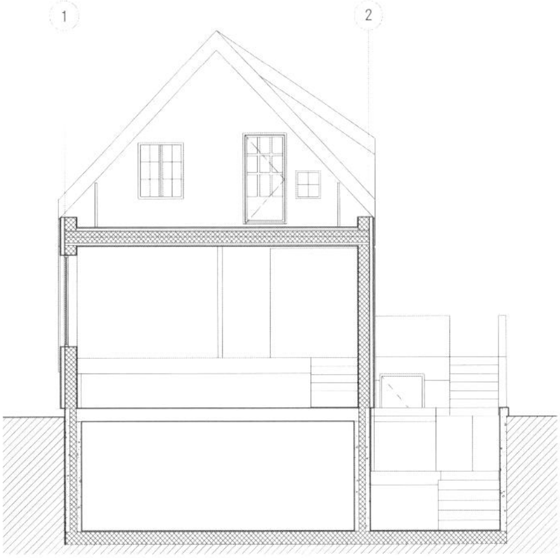

Section 3

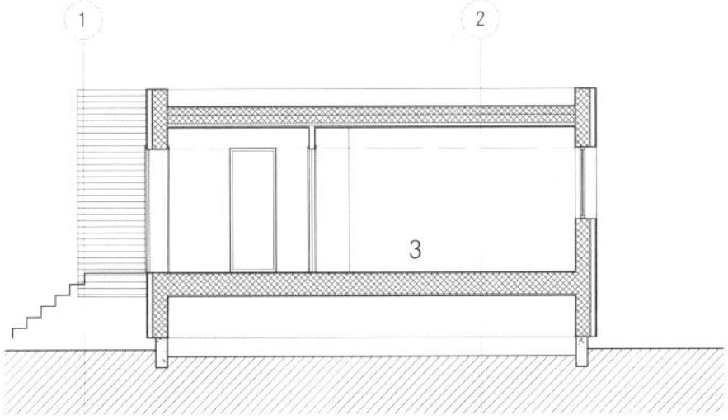

Section 4

1. Roof ventilation through wood boards
2. Heights of ridge and cornice must be as those of existing house
3. New floor at same level as existing

Conceptual rendering

Conceptual scale model

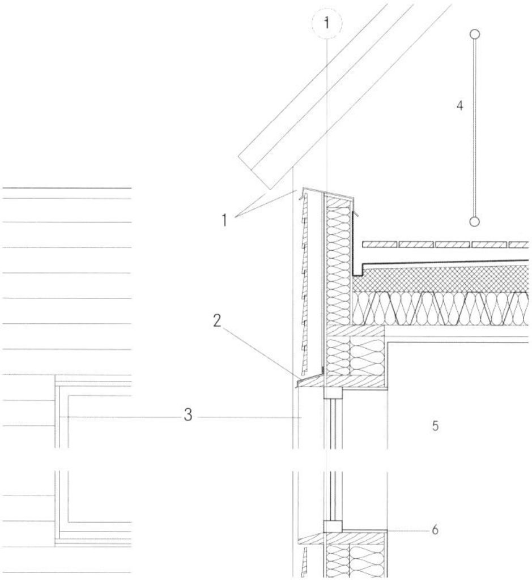

Wall section detail at roof terrace

1. It is important that the highest point of the extension building isn't higher than the lowest point of the existing building's eaves
2. Flashing to be finished in black as unnoticeable as possible
3. Surrounds of window openings (20`110`mm) to be finished to match building cladding
4. Guardrails fastened to building's walls
5. All windows to be set as deep into the walls as possible
6. 12 mm thick interior frame around windows to be painted white to match walls

The steel spiral staircase makes a strong design statement, while connecting all three levels of the addition through a minimal footprint.

Destaca la fuerte presencia de la escalera de caracol de acero que une las tres plantas de la vivienda ocupando una superficie mínima.

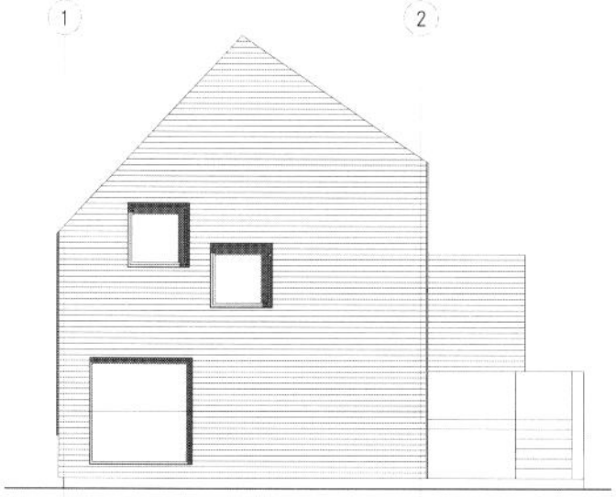

New north elevation

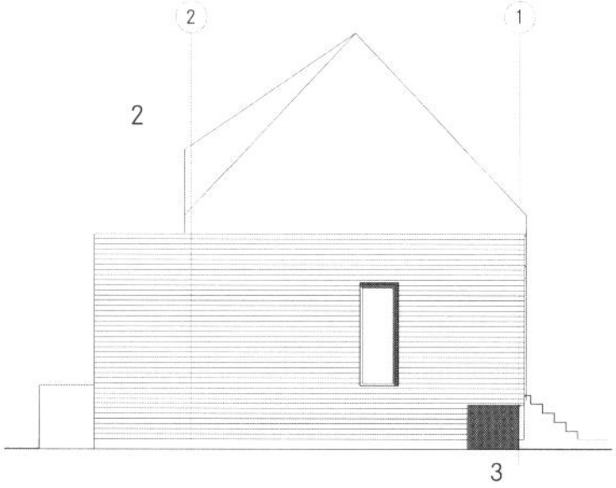

New south elevation

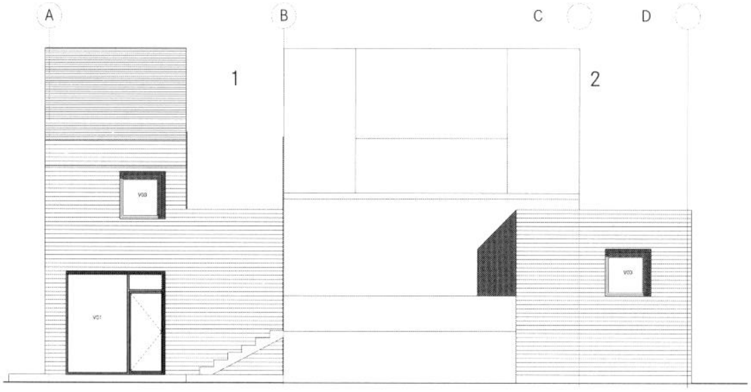

New east elevation

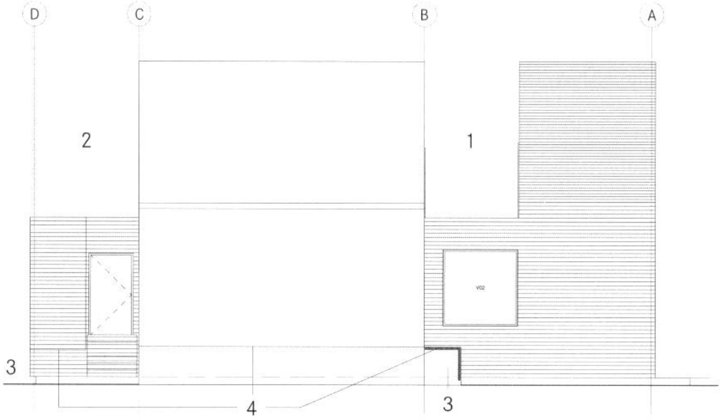

New west elevation

1. Heights of ridge and cornice must be as those of existing house
2. All type V03 windows to be installed as deep into wall from exterior face as possible. All other windows to be installed as close to the exterior face of the wall as possible
3. Cantilever
4. Transition line between cladding and foundation in new construction to be aligned with transition line in existing building

A. Basement room
B. Storage
C. Available space
D. Bathroom
E. Laundry room
F. Lounge
G. Dining area
H. Kitchen
I. Home office
J. Entry
K. Bedroom
L. Terrace
M. Toilet
N. Living area

1. Rough-sawn wood column
2. Foundation under spiral stair and column
3. Maintenance and ventilation hatch
4. Flooring with slope
5. Line of floor above
6. Skylight
7. Space between wall and stairs to accommodate modular sofa (Modern Living)
8. Frosted glass sliding door
9. Integrated TV screen
10. Wood boards to be aligned and mitred when turning corners.
11. Extension cladding starts 40 mm away from existing house cladding

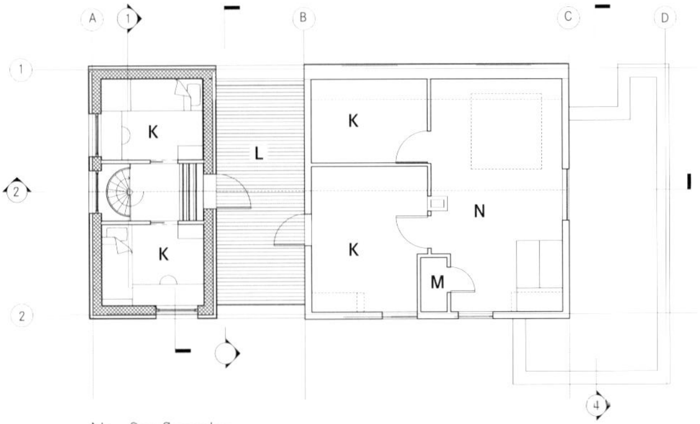

New first floor plan

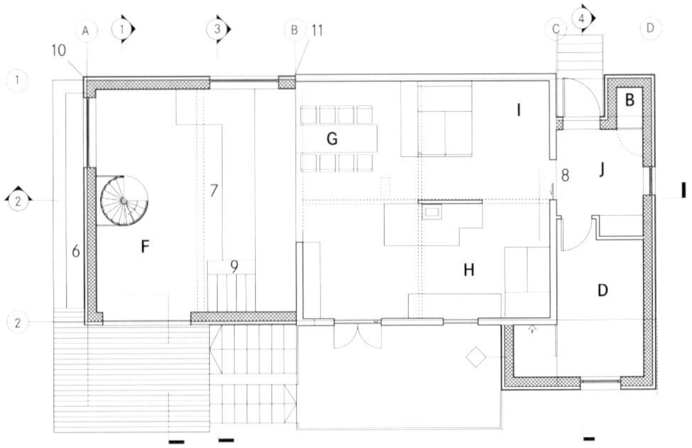

New ground floor plan

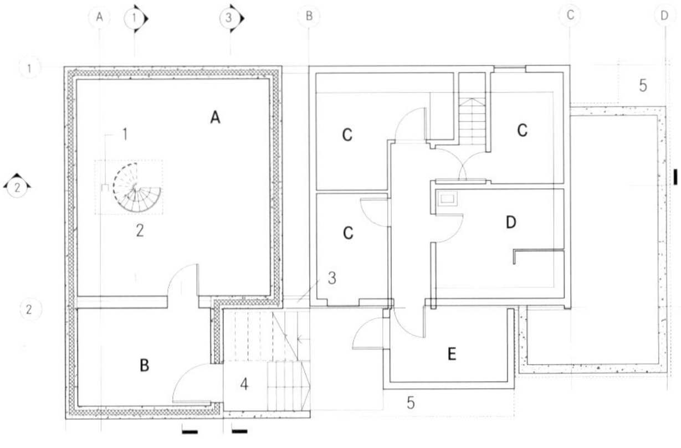

New basement floor plan

The wood surfaces of the extension's interior are given a warm, light tint to achieve an inviting and homely atmosphere, whilst the steel spiral staircase and glass steps add a note of sophistication.

Para lograr un ambiente acogedor y hogareño, se aplicó un tinte claro y cálido a las superficies de madera del interior de la extensión. La nota de sofisticación la añade la escalera de caracol de acero con peldaños de cristal.

AUSTEN HOUSE POD

Flying Contemporary First Floor Extension

Adam Knibb architects

WINCHESTER, HAMPSHIRE, UNITED KINGDOM

Photos © Martin Gardner

Total Building Area: 1765 sq ft – 164 m²
Extension Area: 215 sq ft – 20 m² // 12% of total area

Austen House was a recently converted dwelling on the site of the Old St. Swithun's School. Vacated in 1929, the school had outgrown the city centre location allowing the premises to be taken over by the library and then further development into residential dwellings. Austen House is part of this old development. The owners of the house wanted a clever and creative increase of space as well as abundant natural light and south facing orientation. An access way along one side of the property had to provide a right of passage for cars very occasionally, but it was possible to build out and create a new room over the top of this passage.

Austen House es una vivienda recientemente rehabilitada en el espacio de la escuela Old St. Swithun. La escuela creció hasta superar la capacidad de su ubicación en el centro de la ciudad y se desalojó en 1929. Sus instalaciones las ocuparon en primer lugar, la biblioteca y después se transformaron en viviendas residenciales. Austen House es parte de esta transformación. Los propietarios buscaban una ampliación creativa e inteligente que incorporase mucha luz natural y orientación sur. Una vía de acceso en uno de los lados de la propiedad debía quedar libre para permitir el paso de coches muy ocasionalmente, pero se podía construir por encima y crear una nueva habitación sobre ese pasaje.

Being within the town centre conservation area, the addition to the house had to stand out from the main building with materiality as well as design.

Al estar en la zona de conservación del centro de la ciudad, la ampliación debía diferenciarse del edificio principal por sus materiales y su diseño.

A. Original building
B. Original roof
C. Side accessway

1. PPC aluminium coping
2. Fixed window full height
3. Ceiling bulkhead (internally)
4. Vertical timber cladding units (600 mm bays)
5. Main entrance
6. Skylight (centre of roof)
7. Glazing fixed
8. First floor level
9. New glazed access door
10. Structural vertical slender columns
11. New window to kitchen/dining area to match adjacent windows
12. Boundary west wall to car park

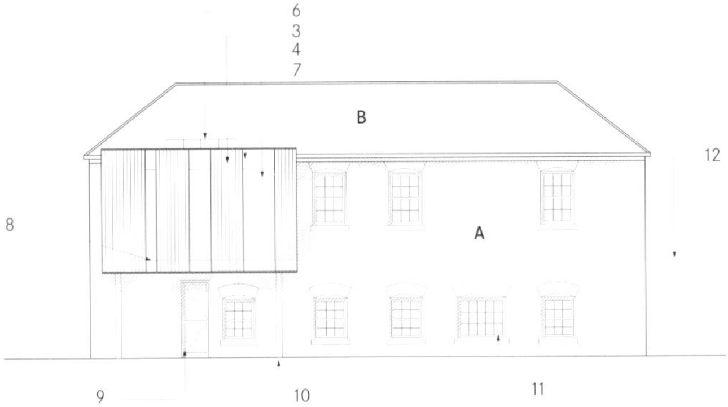

New west elevation

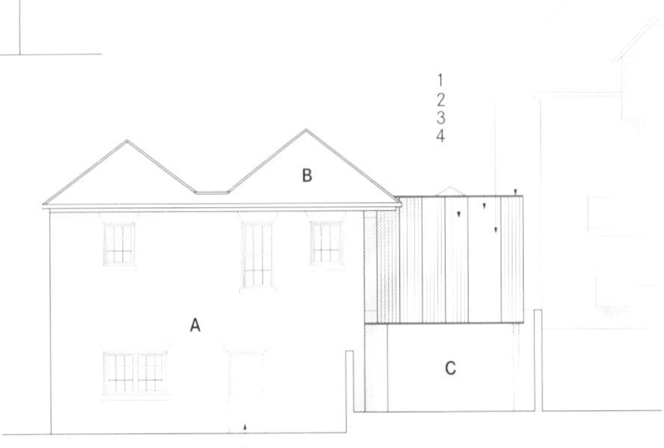

New north elevation

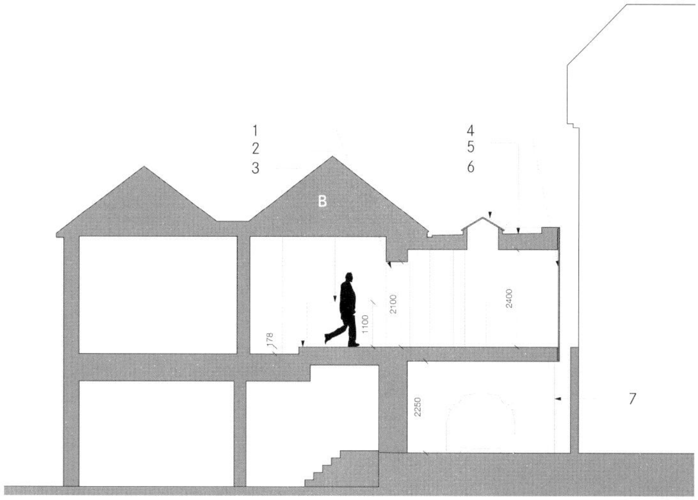

New north section

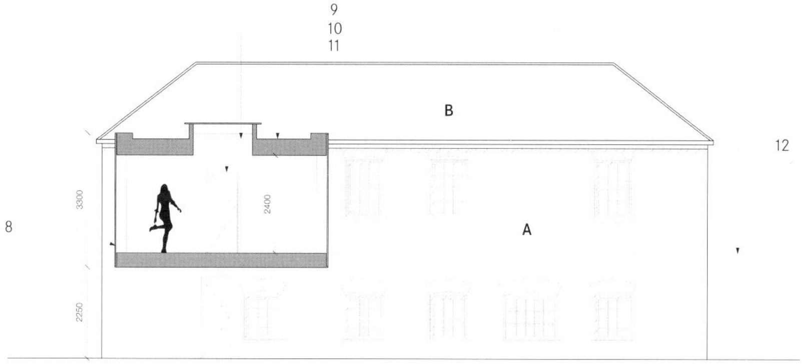

New west section

A. Original building
B. Original roof

1. New internal door
2. Glass balustrade
3. Walkway step up
4. Fixed window full height
5. Flat roof – drainage to existing
6. Skylight/ventilation
7. Slender steel post structure
8. Full height glazing and vertical timber cladding
9. New door way – glazing
10. Skylight
11. Flat roof
12. Boundary west wall to car park

Vertical timber cladding and large sections of glass have been designed to give a greater feeling of verticality and sense of place. With the tight nature of the site, the project was partially completed off-site to ensure minimal disruption.

El recubrimiento en madera con listones verticales y las ventanas alargadas se han diseñado para dar una mayor sensación de verticalidad y de espacio. Debido al limitado espacio del solar, el proyecto se completó parcialmente en fábrica para minimizar molestias en el entorno.

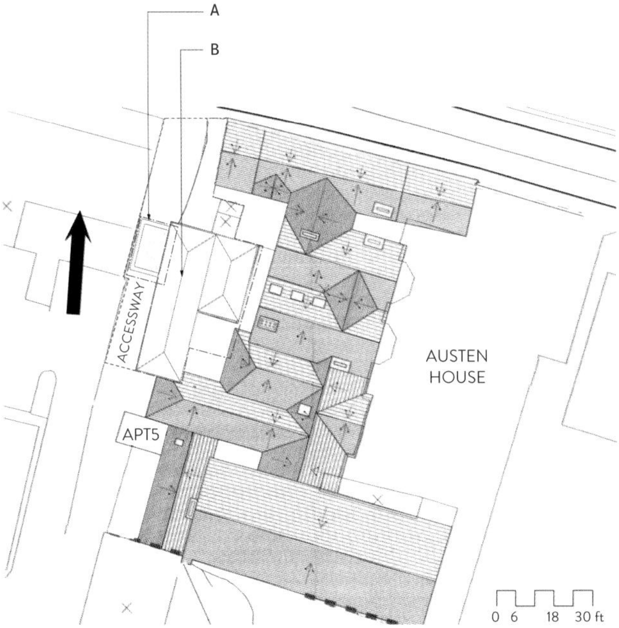

Site plan

A. Proposed extension to Austen House
B. Austen House

-·-·— Site boundary
-·-— Ownership boundary
- - - - Granted rights of use over accessway

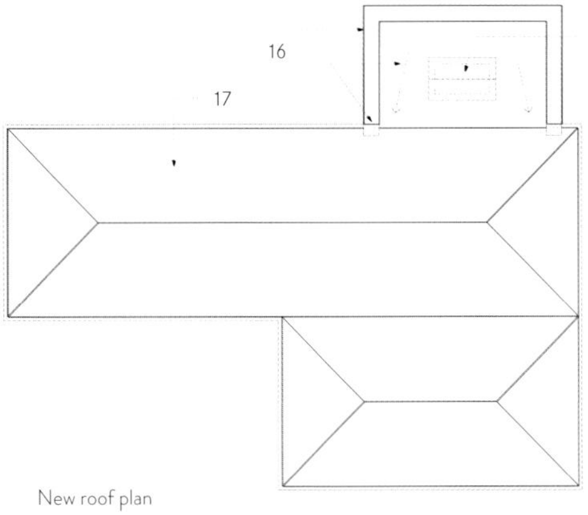

New roof plan

A. Main entrance
B. Hall
C. Lounge
D. Powder room
E. Study
F. Patio
G. Dining area
H. Kitchen
I. Landing
J. Bedroom
K. En suite bathroom
L. Sitting area
M. Bathroom
N. Bedroom

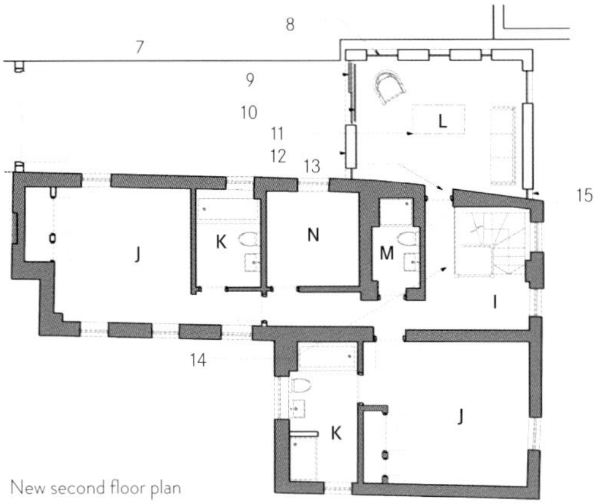

New second floor plan

1. Side access
2. New fixed window
3. Pod structural columns
4. Second floor extension outline above
5. New fully glazed door
6. New opening for door
7. Boundary wall
8. Glazed slot windows
9. Juliet balcony
10. Glass handrail
11. Skylight/ventilation above
12. Solid wall – timber clad
13. New access via full glazed door
14. New bridge walkway – glass handrail
15. Extension touches existing building "lightly" with glass
16. PPC aluminium coping
17. Original tiled pitched roof
18. Skylight with small opening sections for ventilation

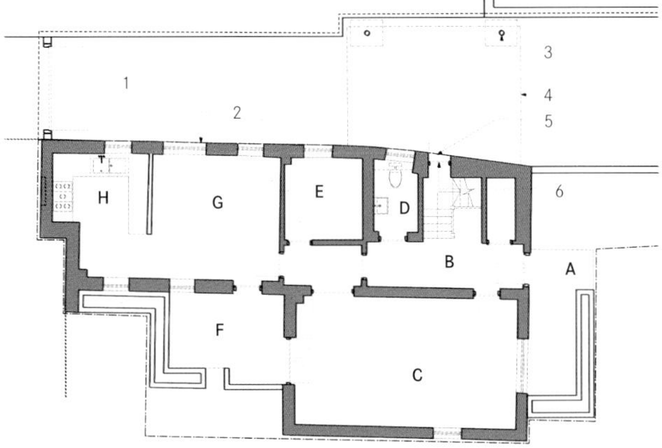

New ground floor plan

Austen House Pod

The floating timber box which touches the building lightly (via glass slot windows) cantilevers out over the access way to give both a dramatic internal space, but also a prominent feature in the neighbourhood.

Unido al edificio central por unas ventanas alargadas, la caja de madera parece flotar sobre el pasaje de entrada para crear un espacio interior sorprendente, pero sobre todo una característica distintiva al barrio.

KENWORTHY HOUSE

Rethinking the family home

Chris Dyson architects

LONDON, UNITED KINGDOM

Photos © Peter Landers

Total Building Area: 1916 sq ft – 178 m^2
Extension Area: 1108 sq ft – 103 m^2 // 58% of total area

An existing narrow closet wing was demolished and rebuilt as a lightweight, highly insulated timber frame construction. A double height glazed screen indicates the new entry point and gives a clear visual separation between the old part of the house and the new. A loft conversion clad in the same material completes the extension of the accommodation. The finished building provides the family with spacious, bright bedrooms; a large family kitchen with breakfast and dining area that opens up to the garden; and a striking, modern piece of architecture that complements the existing building.

Se demolió una estrecha ampliación existente en la parte de atrás y se erigió de nuevo como una construcción ligera, que destaca por el uso de la madera y su gran aislamiento. Una apertura de cristal a doble altura indica el nuevo punto de entrada y otorga una clara separación entre la parte antigua y la nueva de la casa. La transformación de la buhardilla recubierta del mismo material completa la ampliación de la vivienda. El edificio resultante proporciona a la familia dormitorios espaciosos y luminosos, una gran cocina con zona de desayuno y un comedor abierto al jardín; una pieza arquitectónica, moderna y llamativa que complementa el edificio original.

30

The entrance to the house was relocated to the centre of the plan, providing a dramatic entry into the heart of the house, whilst freeing up the previous entry position to be used as an entry-level water closet.

La entrada se reubicó en el centro del plano para conseguir un espectacular acceso al corazón de la vivienda, a la vez que libera la antigua entrada para convertirse en un baño en la planta baja.

1. Charred cedar timber weatherboarding
2. Artificial slate
3. PPC aluminium framed window
4. Double glazed panel
5. Glazed entrance screen
6. Reused sliding sash window
7. Existing garden wall
8. Aluminium bifold door
9. Painted render
10. Lower panes to be covered with translucent film
11. Lower area of glass to be translucent/obscure
12. Existing garden door repainted
13. Extension below existing eaves line
14. Concealed gutter detail
15. Existing window opening filled and rendered
16. Minimal flashing to edge of timber

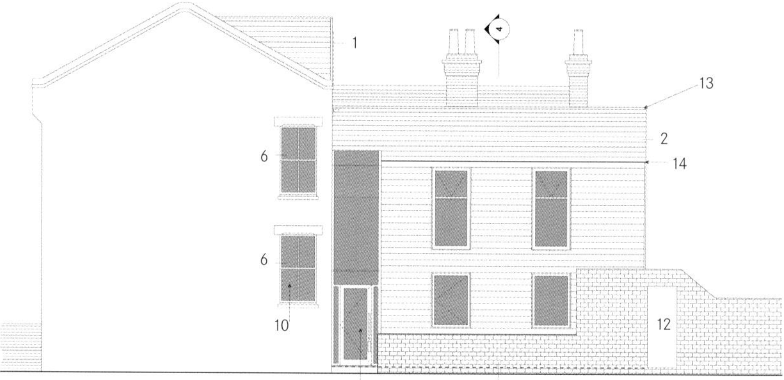

New side elevation

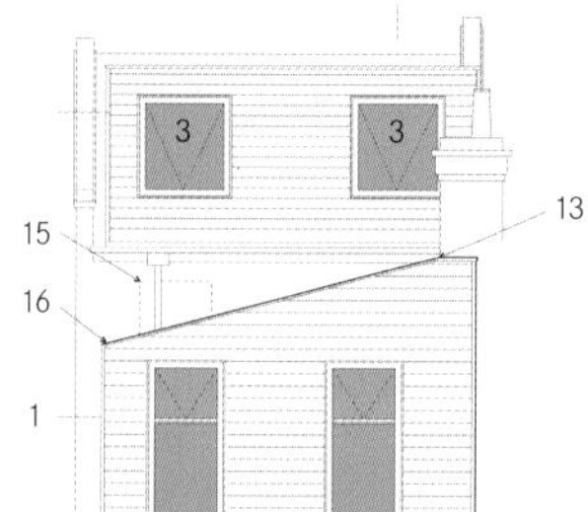

New rear elevation

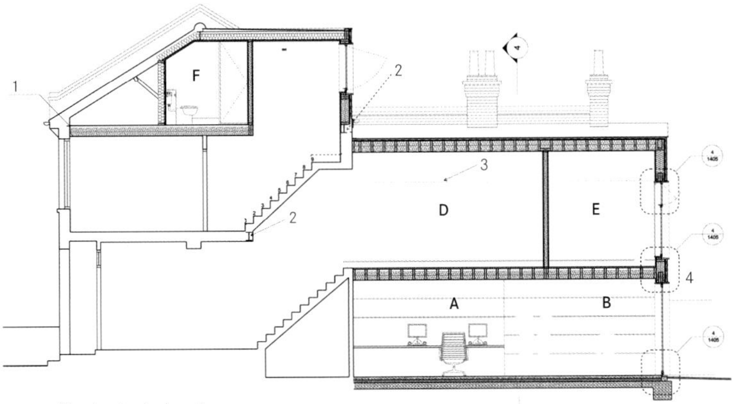

New longitudinal section

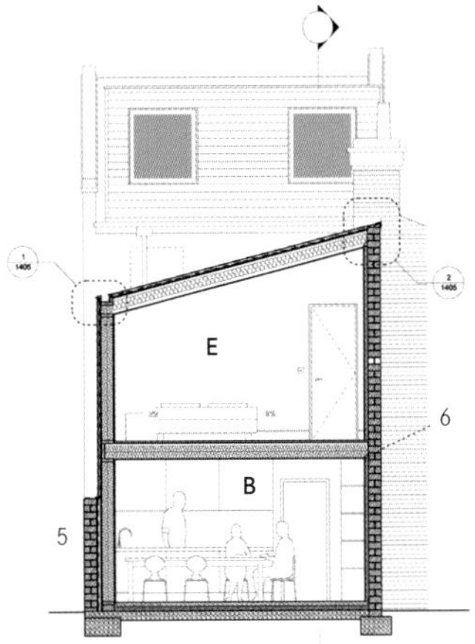

New cross section

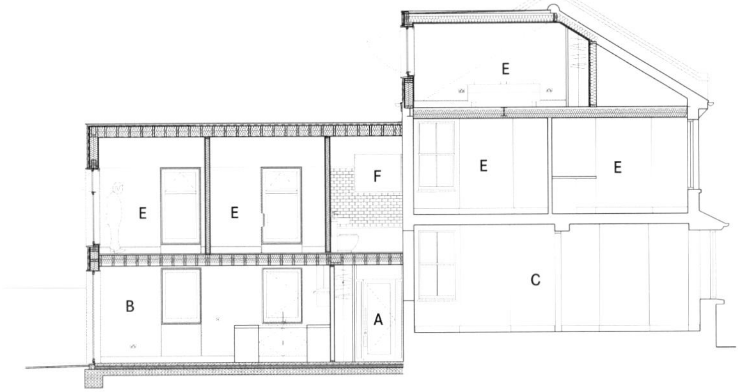

New longitudinal section

0 2 4 6 8 10 m

A. Study area
B. Kitchen/dining room
C. Living room
D. Hallway
E. Bedroom
F. Bathroom

1. New floor joists to bear on heavy duty joist hangers subject to suitability of existing lintels
2. Steel beam to structural engineer's specification
3. Ceiling at lowest level
4. Structural timber lintel 2 No 250 x 50
5. Existing wall rebuilt on new footing
6. New floor joists to bear on heavy duty joist hangers

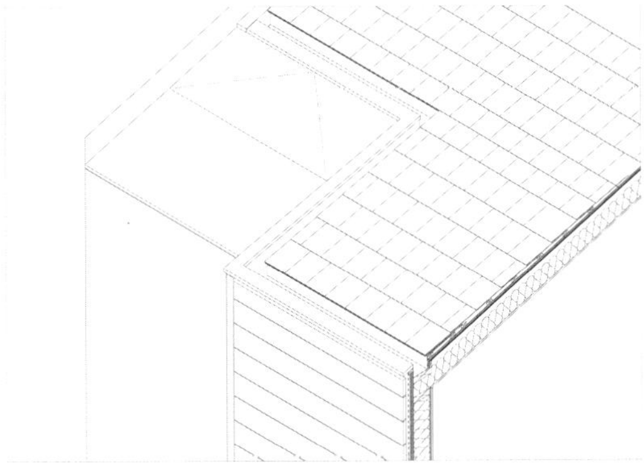

Isometric view of roof construction

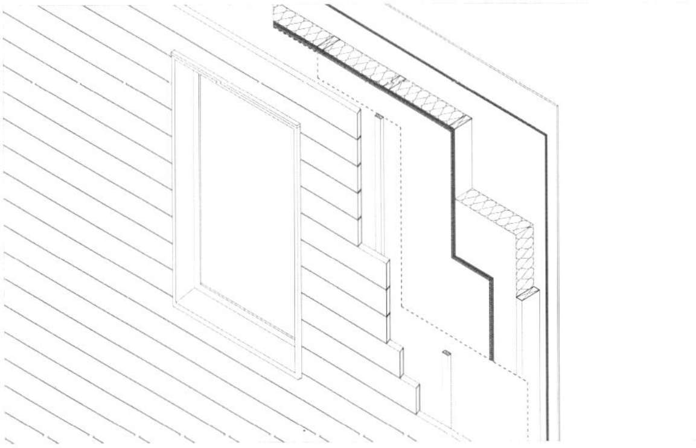

Isometric view of new wall construction

The extension and the loft are clad with charred cedar boards, which beautifully complement the Victorian brickwork of the surrounding context and give the extension a firm legibility as a modern intervention.

La ampliación y la buhardilla están revestidas con placas de madera de cedro oscuro, que complementan el ladrillo victoriano que la rodea, y le da la legitimidad de una intervención moderna.

A. Entrance
B. Garden
C. Living room
D. Powder room
E. Hall
F. Study area
G. Kitchen/dining area
H. Bedroom
I. Bathroom

1. 1100 high brick wall
2. Gate
3. Planting
4. 950 high brick wall
5. New drainage connections, new manhole location to be determined on site
6. Gas meter
7. Rainwater pipe
8. Retained front door form. New insulated studwork
9. New WC
10. Retained sash window and lintel in new opening
11. Glazed entrance screen
12. Void above
13. Existing garden wall partially rebuilt. New insulated timber weatherboard set behind
14. Existing garden door
15. Aluminium folding door system
16. Slot drain
17. Neighbouring window
18. 45 degrees line from centre
19. Existing slate roof
20. Timber weatherboard wall
21. Glazed roof
22. Party wall raised in brick to allow neighbour to construct loft extension
23. Artificial slate roof
24. Concealed downpipe discharging into new concealed gutter
25. GRP flat roof to fall toward parapet

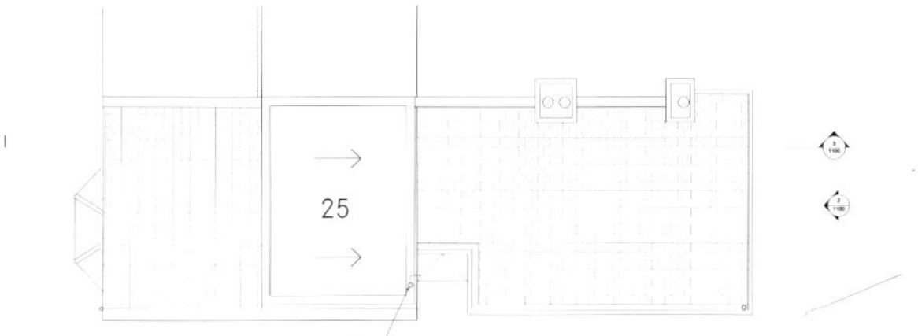

New roof plan

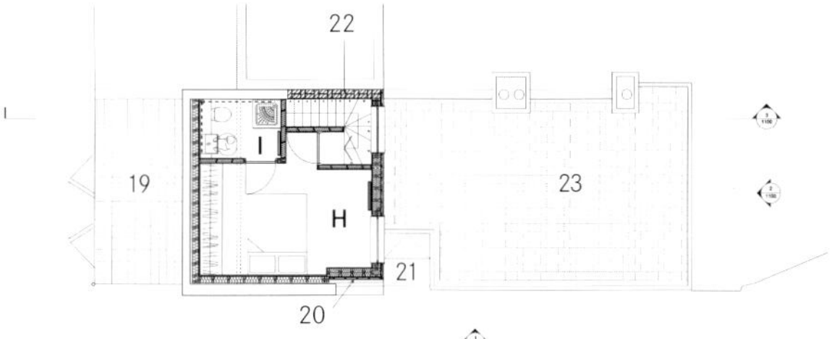

New second floor plan

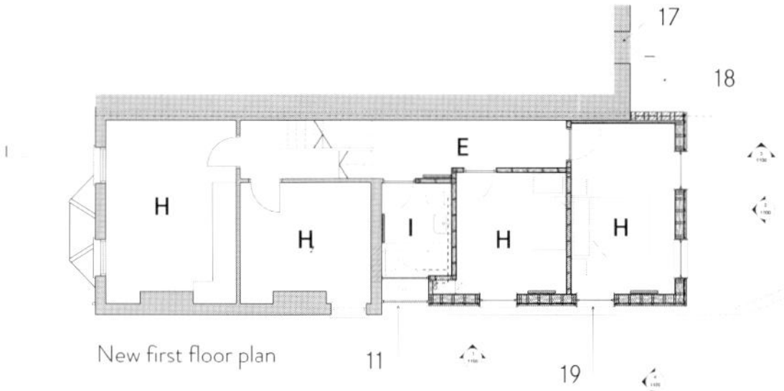

New first floor plan

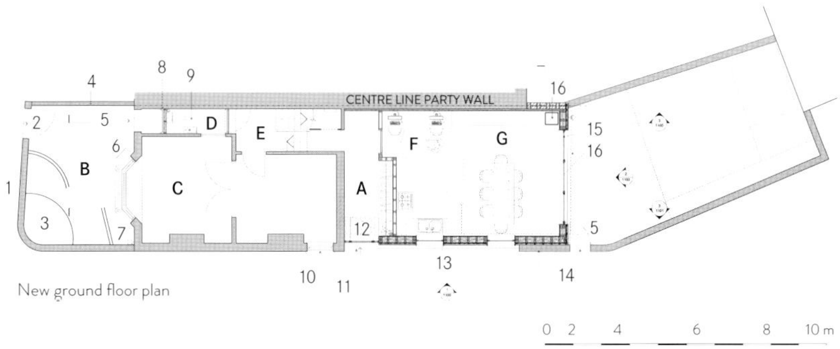

New ground floor plan

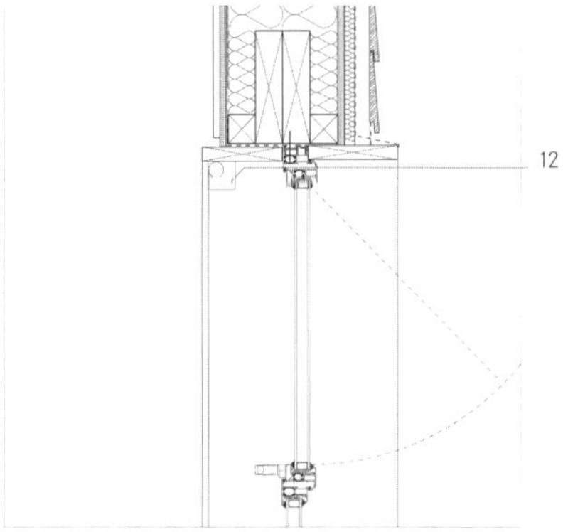

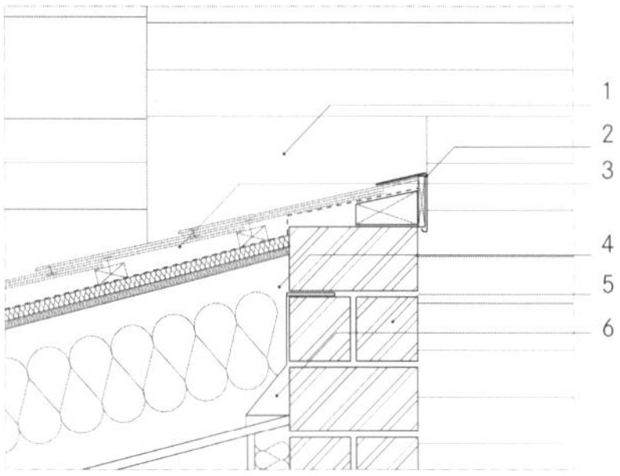

Ridge detail

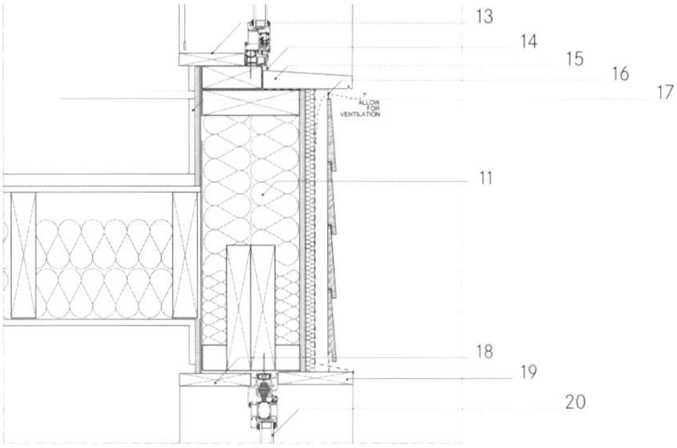

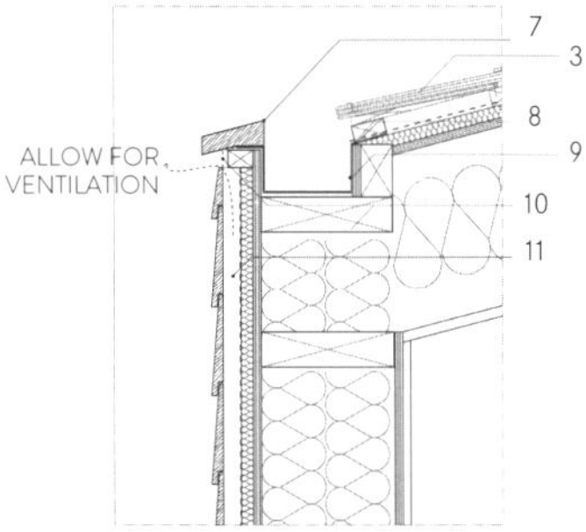

Concealed gutter detail

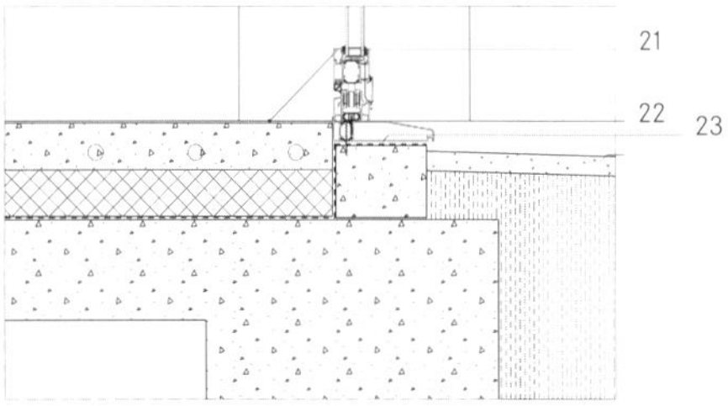

Garden door and window details

1. Code 4 lead flashing to perimeter chased into mortar joint 150 mm above roof level
2. Code 4 lead flashing drip detail over fascia
3. - Marley eternity slates
   - Tanalised SW battens
   - Proclima Solitex WA breather membrane
   - 18 mm WBP plywood
   - 165 mm Celotex XR4000 between rafters
   - Proclima intrlloplus VCL
   - 12.5 mm plasterboard, skim finish
4. Wrap rafters ends in DPC
5. Reclaimed brick party wall extension tied back to existing with starter bars
6. Heavy duty joist hangers built into wall
7. Solid charred cedar coping
8. Breather membrane lapped into gutter
9. Code 4 lead formed gutter on WBP plywood
10. Insect closing ventilated cavity
11. - Charred cedar cladding fixed to battens with sheradised hidden head annular ring shank nails
    - Tanalised SW battens forming ventilated cavity closed top and bottom with insect mesh
    - Proclima Solitex WA breather membrane
    - 25 mm Celotex FR5000 mechanically fixed
    - WBP plywood sheathing
    - Celotex FR4000 between studs
    - Proclima Intelloplus VCL
    - 12 mm plywood
    - 12.5 mm wallboard, skim finish
12. Roller blind fitting
13. Natural cedar internal reveal
14. Silicone seal
15. Natural cedar sill with drip throat cut breather membrane lapped underneath
16. Insect mesh
17. MDF skirting
18. Natural cedar internal reveal, broken around door fixing
19. Natural cedar reveal, breather membrane lapped over top
20. Bifolding timber door
21. - 3 mm poured resin
    - 70 mm screed with UFH heating
    - Isolating membrane
    - Bituthene PDM
    - Slab to engineers spec
22. Bituthene DPM lapped under door threshold
23. Gravel external finish

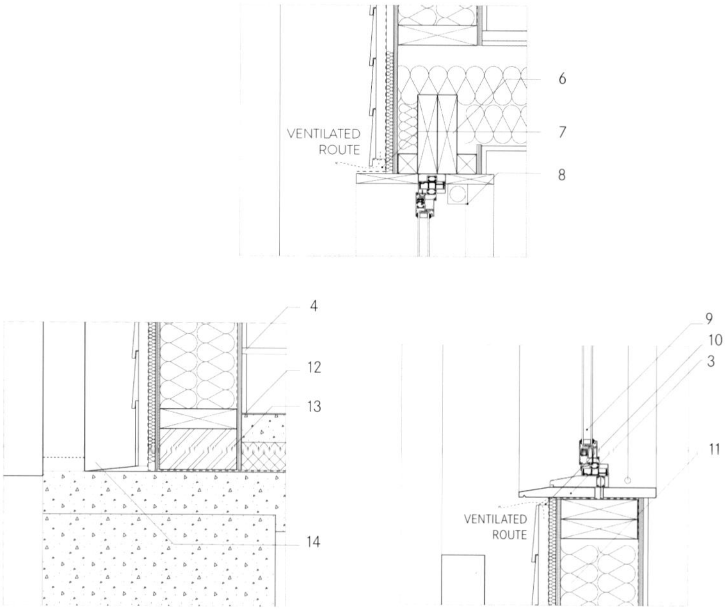

Window section detail

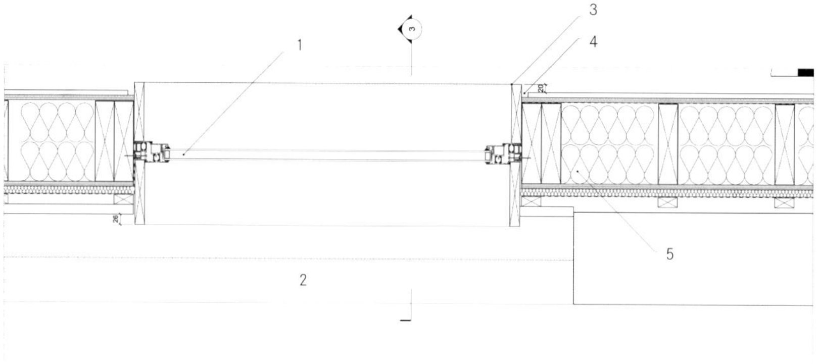

Typical window plan detail

1. PPC aluminium double glazed window
2. Garden wall below
3. Natural cedar window sill
4. 15 mm shadow gap trim
5. - Plasterboard, skim finish
   - 12 mm plywood
   - Intelloplus VCL, joints taped
   - Insulation between studs
   - 12 mm WBP plywood
   - Rigid insulation
   - Proclima Solitex WA breather membrane
   - Tanalised SW battens forming ventilated cavity
   - Charred cedar cladding
6. 2/200 x 50 C 24 joists bolted together
7. Lead flashing to top of cedar trim
8. Roller blind system
9. Proprietary aluminium double glazed window
10. Insect mesh to ventilated cavity
11. - Charred cedar cladding fixed to battens with sheradised hidden head annular ring shank nails
    - Tanalised SW battens forming ventilated cavity closed top and bottom with insect mesh
    - Proclima Solitex WA breather membrane
    - 25 mm Celotex FR5000 Mechanically fixed
    - WBP plywood sheathing
    - Celotex FR4000 between studs
    - Proclima Intelloplus VCL
    - 12 mm plywood
    - 12.5 mm plasterboard, skim finish
13. - 3 mm resin floor
    - 70 mm screed with UFH pipes
    - 60 mm insulation
    - Bituthene DPM
    - Structural RC slab
14. Weep holes to base of wall and code 4 lead flashing weathered under base of timber cladding

On the upper floor, the ceiling in the rooms follows the pitch of the roof, giving the spaces additional height and volume. Large format windows flood the rooms with light.

En el piso superior, el techo de las habitaciones sigue la inclinación del tejado, otorgando a las estancias mayor altura y volumen. Las ventanas de gran tamaño inundan de luz el interior.

CUT AND FRAME

Home Extension and Writing Studio

Ashton Porter architects

LONDON, UNITED KINGDOM

Photos © Andy Stagg

Total Building Area: 1916 sq ft – 178 m^2
Extension Area: 323 sq ft – 30 m^2 // 17% of total area

This extension must be understood as a visual connection between an existing two-storey semi-detached house and a former garden shed at the rear of the garden transformed into a writing hut. The design was driven by the requirements from the clients, a couple working from home, but with different occupations, one client being a children's book author, the other, a therapist. They both wanted separate spaces but somewhat connected. The tie between the house and the garden writing hut was therefore a key element of the project.

Esta ampliación debe comprenderse como una conexión visual entre una casa pareada de dos plantas y un antiguo cobertizo de jardín en la parte de atrás del mismo, transformado en un refugio para la escritura. El diseño se realizó teniendo en cuenta los deseos de los clientes: una pareja que trabajaba desde casa pero con distintas profesiones: escritor de libros infantiles y terapeuta. Ambos querían espacios separados pero conectados de algún modo. Por ello, el nexo entre la casa y el refugio de escritura del jardín fue un elemento clave del proyecto.

The interior of the existing house was completely remodelled and a series of historical, compartmentalised additions and alterations were removed to provide improved, interconnected living spaces.

El interior de la casa existente se remodeló completamente. Se eliminaron una serie de adiciones y alteraciones anteriores que dividían el espacio, para ofrecer unos espacios comunes mejorados e interconectados.

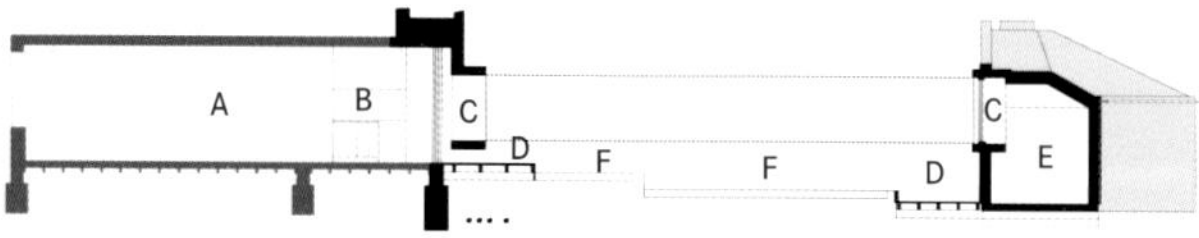

New section AA

A. Living room
B. Kitchen
C. Window seat
D. Red cedar decking
E. Writing hut
F. Lawn

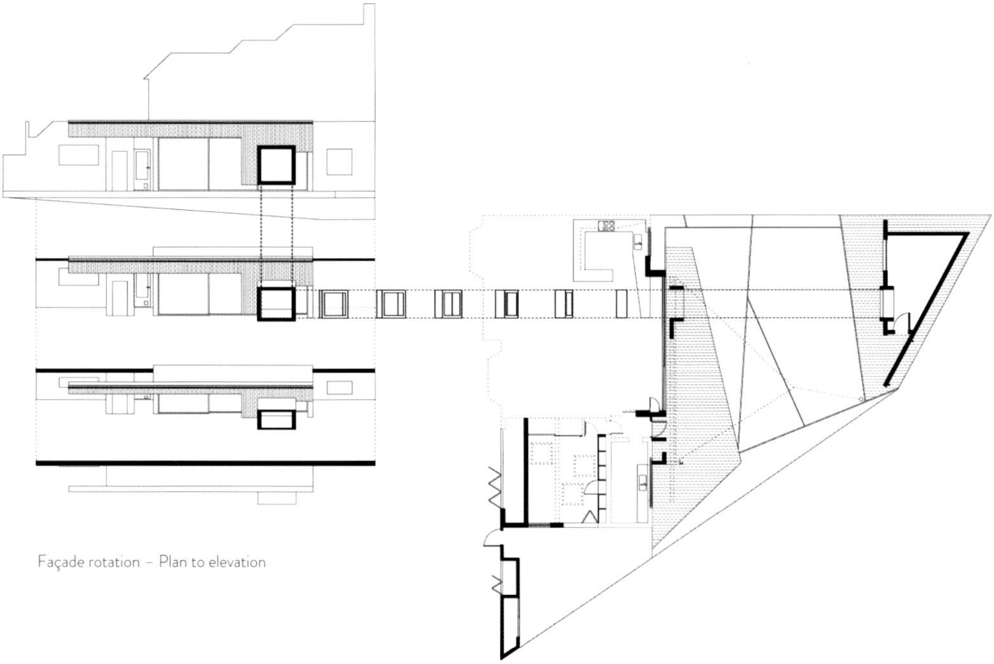

Façade rotation – Plan to elevation

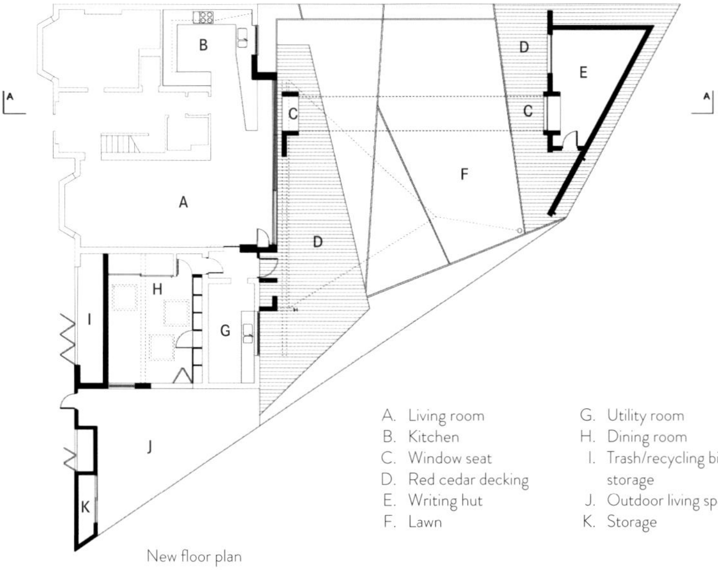

A. Living room
B. Kitchen
C. Window seat
D. Red cedar decking
E. Writing hut
F. Lawn
G. Utility room
H. Dining room
I. Trash/recycling bins storage
J. Outdoor living space
K. Storage

New floor plan

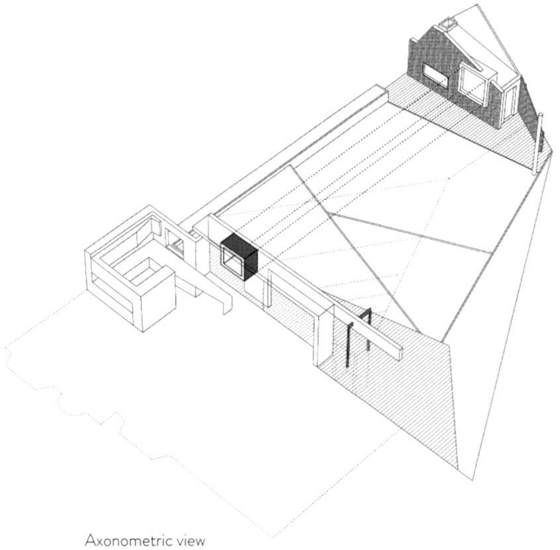

Axonometric view

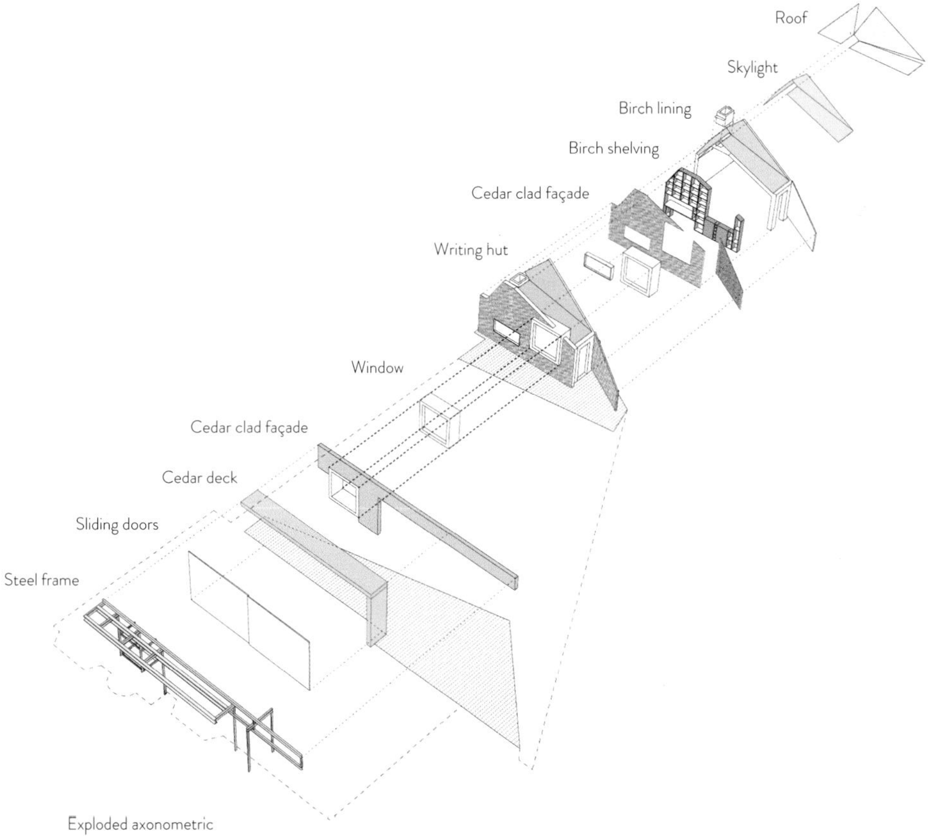

Exploded axonometric

Framing elements reinforce the connection between hut and home. The main house has a floating seat of aluminium that becomes part of the internal seating of the house when the large glazed panels are slid away, and a garden seat at all times.

Los perfiles refuerzan la conexión entre el refugio y la casa. La vivienda principal tiene un banco flotante de aluminio que forma parte del mobiliario interior cuando se abren los grandes paneles acristalados, mientras que puede usarse como banco de jardín en todo momento.

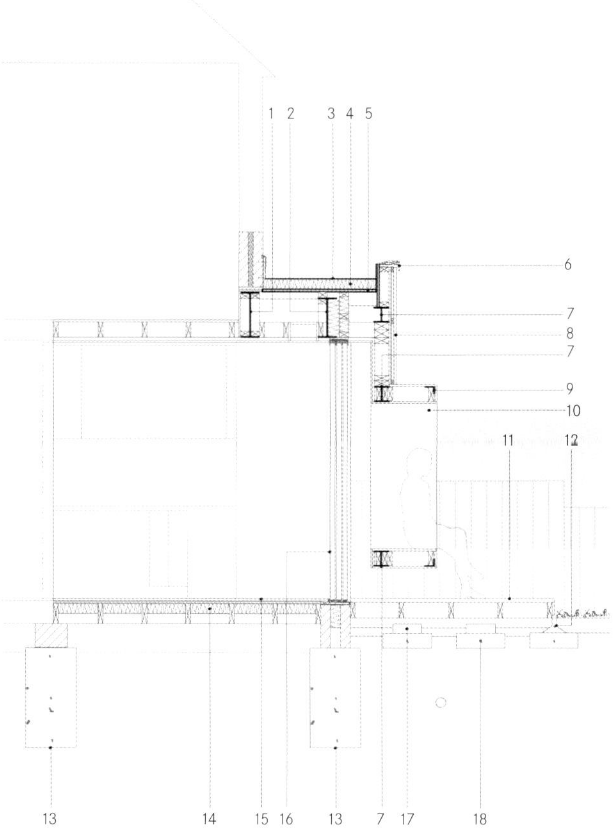

Building section detail

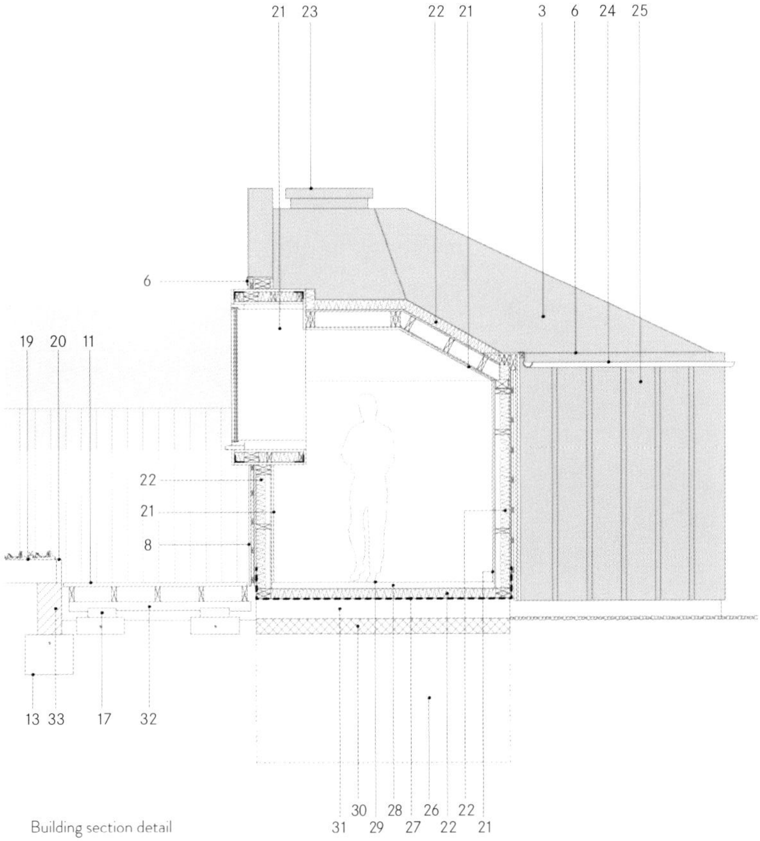

Building section detail

1. 457 x 191 x 67 UB.
2. 406 x 178 x 67 UB.
3. Fiberglass roof in dark grey finish
4. 120 mm PIR Celotex XR4000
5. 18 mm WBP plywood
6. Fiberglass edge trim with lead grey finish
7. 152 mm uc frame
8. 100 x 20 cedar cladding with bevel cut to both edges
9. Angle frame to form seat
10. 3 mm aluminium sheet
11. 40 x 90 m western red cedar decking
12. 50 x 150 precast concrete edging set in concrete benching
13. New in situ mass concrete foundation
14. 100 mm PIR XR4000 insulation
15. Oak floor boards
16. Grey powder coated aluminium sliding doors
17. Precast concrete foundation pad
18. Gravel base
19. New horizontal terraced garden laid to lawn
20. 63 x 220 mm oak plan 2.6 m long) edging
21. 12 mm birch-faced lining
22. 100 mm styrene insulation
23. Grey powder coated aluminium skylight
24. 135 PVC half round gutter system (1:60 fall) in grey
25. Ebony stained 18 mm wbp cladding with external sw battens to vertical joints
26. In situ mass concrete lateral strips
27. Damp proof membrane
28. 65 mm sand cement screed
29. Rubber floor
30. Compressible board
31. In situ mass concrete slab with reinforcement mesh
32. Tanalised softwood joists
33. Masonry retaining wall

JACK'S HOUSE

An extension in dialogue with a victorian terrace and an industrial warehouse

FMD architects

MELBOURNE, AUSTRALIA

Photos © Shannon McGrath

Total Building Area: 1937 sq ft – 180 m^2
Extension Area: 581 sq ft – 54 m^2 // 30% of total area

The new extension offers a dialogue between two buildings of different eras, disconnected in style and function: an existing Victorian residence facing the street and an industrial saw-tooth warehouse on the rear boundary. The extension negotiates between the two buildings, stretching and tapering toward the saw-tooth brick building. Internally, it opens up from a double-loaded Victorian corridor to a spacious glazed room, with a brick wall on the boundary as a feature backdrop.
The existing street frontage was maintained without alteration, in keeping with the local character of hidden extensions to the rear of existing houses.

La nueva extensión ofrece un diálogo entre dos edificios de distintos tiempos, desconectados en estilo y función: una residencia victoriana original junto a la calle y un almacén industrial con tejado en diente de sierra en la parte trasera de la propiedad. La extensión sirve de nexo entre los dos edificios, estirándose y estrechándose conforme se acerca al edificio industrial de ladrillo. Internamente, se abre desde un pasillo victoriano con puertas a ambos lados a una espaciosa habitación acristalada y con una pared de ladrillo en la linde como telón de fondo distintivo.
La fachada a la calle se conservó sin alteraciones, manteniendo el carácter local de esconder las extensiones en la parte de atrás de las casas originales.

Jack's House

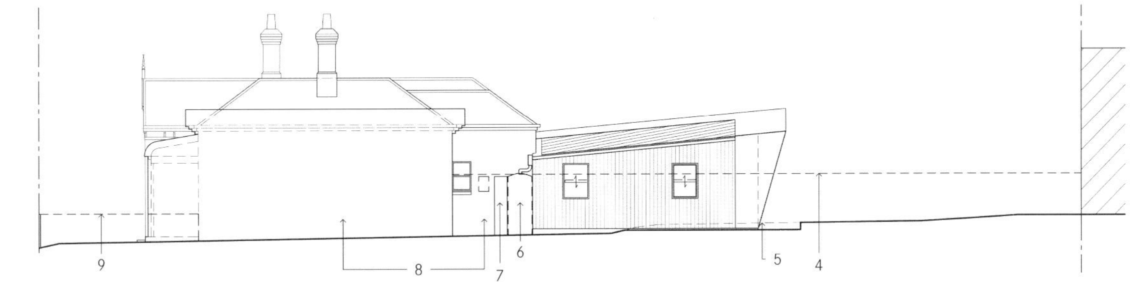

New south elevation

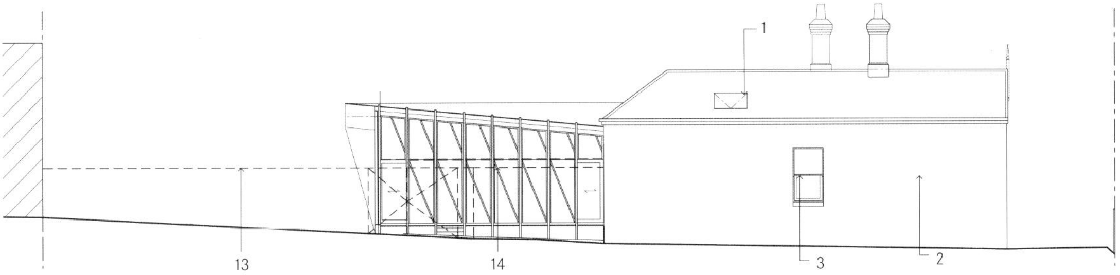

New north elevation

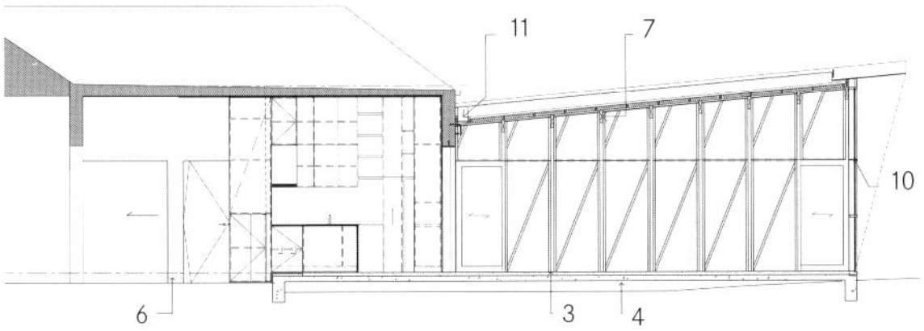

New partial longitudinal section

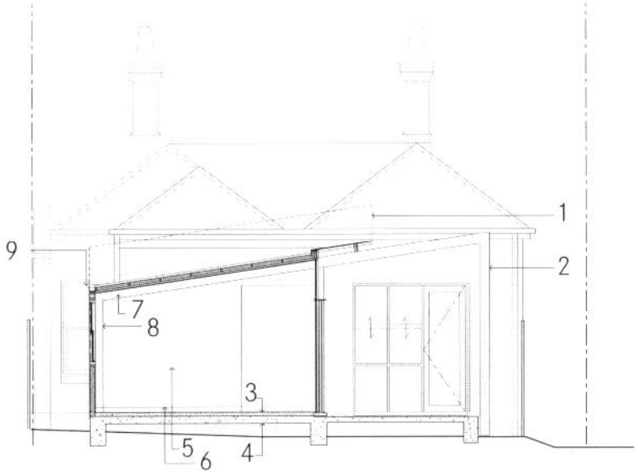

Cross section

— · — · — · — Boundary line

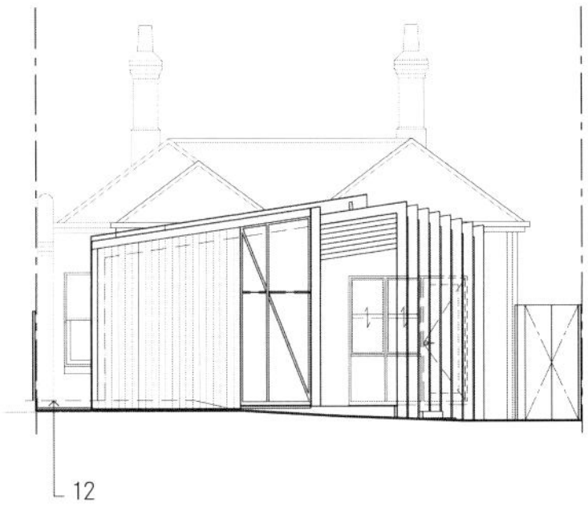

New east elevation

New west elevation

1. Canopy in front
2. Timber column to engineer's specifications
3. 70 mm topping slab for hydronic heating
4. Structural slab
5. Direct stick plaster to existing
6. Skirting as specified
7. Timber beam to engineer's details
8. Timber post (non-structural)
9. Rainwater head beyond
10. Steel angle lintel
11. Soaker gutter
12. Natural ground line shown dashed
13. Original fence
14. New fencing

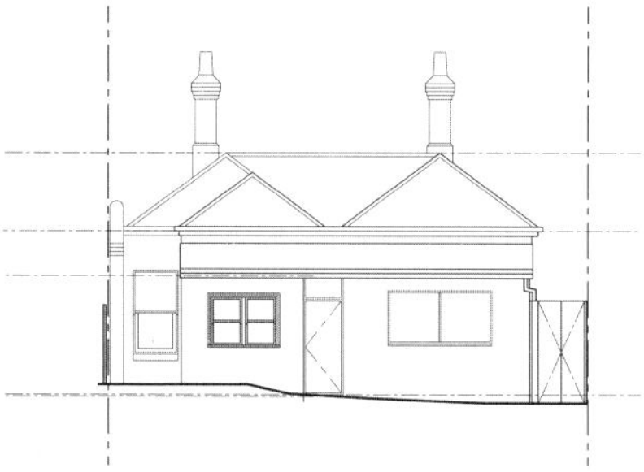

Original east elevation

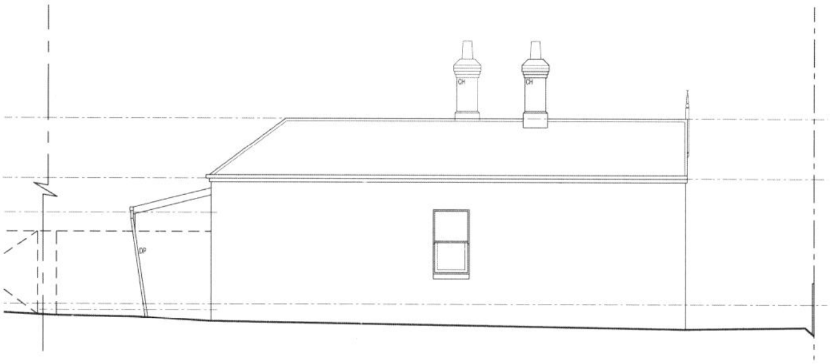

Original north elevation

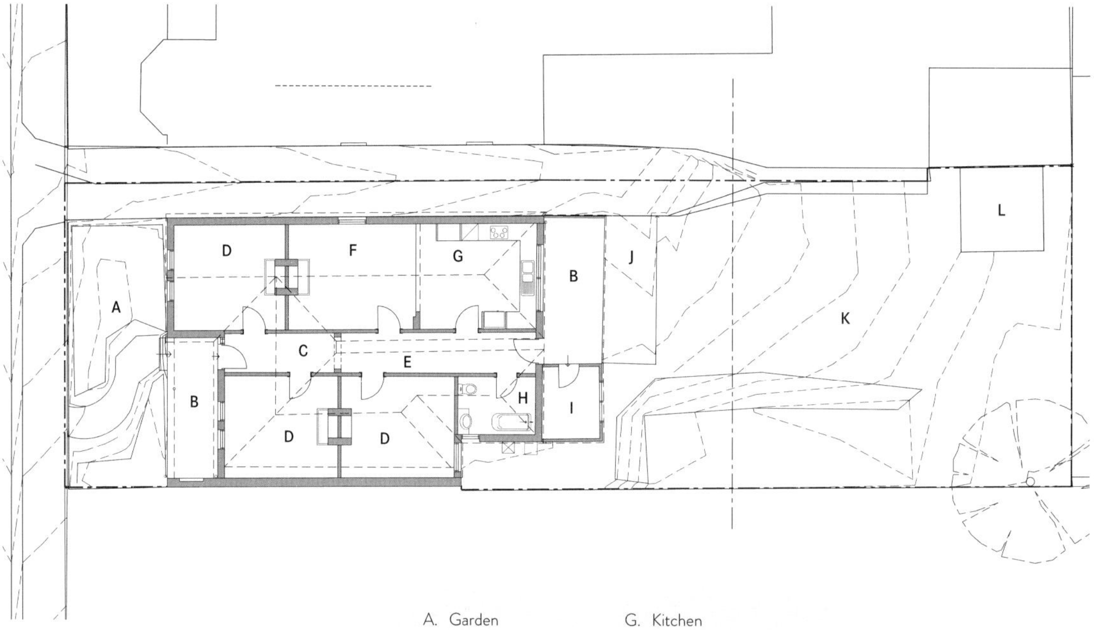

Original floor plan

A. Garden
B. Veranda
C. Entry
D. Bedroom
E. Hall
F. Lounge
G. Kitchen
H. Bathroom
I. Laundry room
J. Paved area
K. Grass backyard
L. Galvanized iron shed

Re-planning of the existing interior allowed the floor plan to improve its efficiency, thus ensuring the footprint of the new extension was minimized and the garden maximized.

La replanificación del espacio interior permitió que el plano mejorase su eficiencia, asegurando que el espacio de la extensión se minimizara y el jardín se maximizara.

Original west elevation

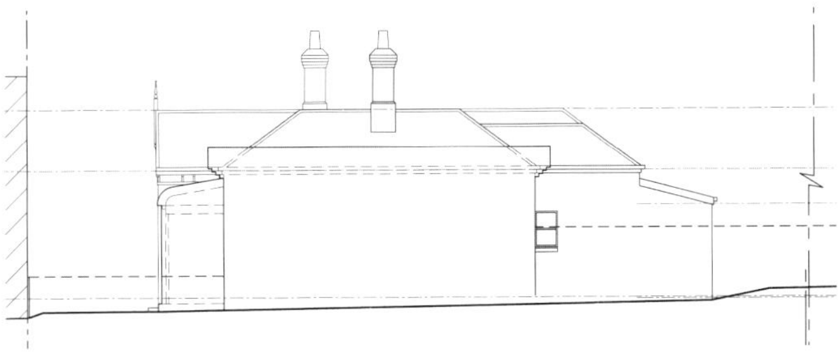

Original south elevation

— - — - — - — Boundary line

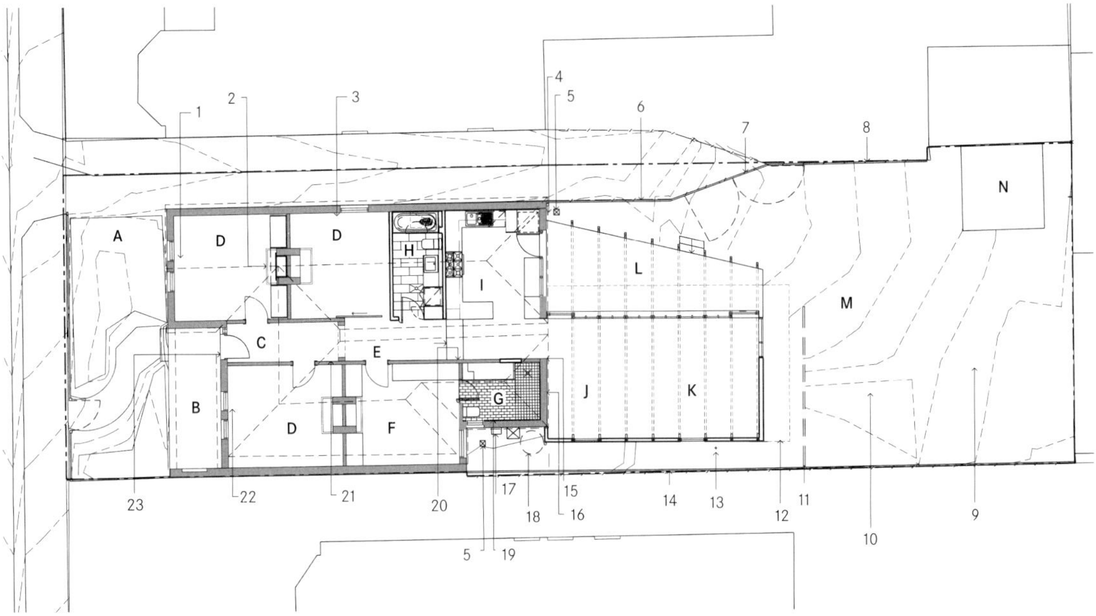

New floor plan

1. Boards retained for re-use
2. CT-06 to hearth
3. Patch and conceal existing A/C pipework
4. New tap
5. New storm water pit
6. New 2.5 m high paling fence (height to match existing)
7. Existing gate
8. Existing fence
9. Clothes line position to be confirmed
10. Site level to be confirmed
11. Retaining wall and AGI drain to be confirmed
12. Cantilevered canopy over
13. Relocated tap
14. Retaining wall to be confirmed
15. Patch plaster where nib removed
16. New sheet plaster over stud wall
17. New hot water system
18. New tank (by client)
19. New sheet plaster over stud wall
20. New skirting to match existing and follow line of step
21. Conceal thermostat conduit and patch as required
22. Patch flooring with retained boards
23. New weather strike to perimeter of existing door

A. Garden
B. Veranda
C. Entry
D. Bedroom
E. Hall
F. Master bedroom
G. Master bathroom
H. Bathroom
I. Kitchen
J. Dining area
K. Lounge area
L. Terrace
M. Grass backyard
N. Existing galvanized shed

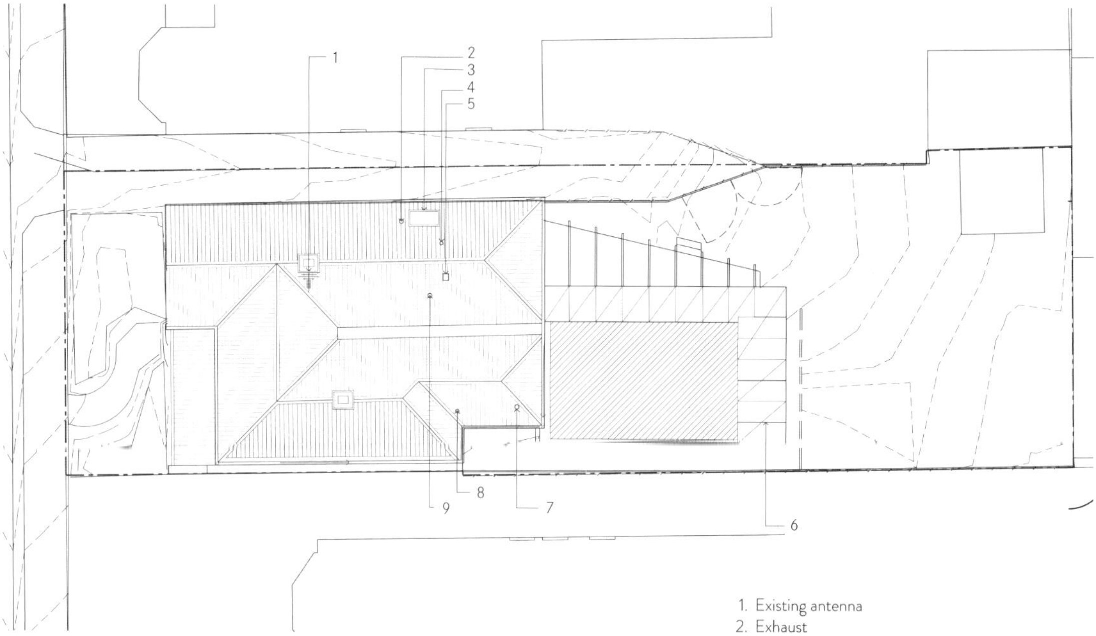

New roof plan

1. Existing antenna
2. Exhaust
3. New skylight as specified
4. Toilet vent
5. Range hood exhaust
6. Stiffeners to east canopy to engineer's specifications
7. Existing exhaust
8. Toilet vent
9. Dryer exhaust

The extension allows the Victorian house to open itself up to natural light and ventilation and provide a large open plan living and dining area. The kitchen is also renovated and repositioned to improve its connection with the garden.

La extensión permite que la casa victoriana se abra a la luz natural y la ventilación a la vez que proporciona una gran área abierta para el comedor y zona de estar. La cocina también se renovó y reinstaló para mejorar su conexión con el jardín.

The interior detailing transitions from the Victorian craftsmanship to the modern plywood detailing as on moves through the spaces.

Conforme nos movemos por las estancias observamos el cambio de los detalles artesanales victorianos a los remates modernos en contrachapado.

JIMI HOUSE

A home for art

Paul Archer design

LONDON, UNITED KINGDOM

Photos © Alexander James and Paul Archer

Total Building Area: 1938 sq ft – 180 m²
Extension Area: 43 sq ft – 4 m² // 2.5% of total area

The remodel and extension of a Victorian terraced house opens up its interior spaces to the garden, brings in daylight, and provides clear sight lines for the display of the owners' art collection. The added space neatly accommodates a modern light-filled galley kitchen with openings into a new spacious dining area and access to the garden. A clear layout and various design elements such as a full height glazed pivot door and glass balustrade on the upper ground level establish visual connections between the different spaces as well as between the interior and the exterior.

La remodelación y ampliación de una casa adosada victoriana abre su espacio interior al jardín, atrae la luz natural y proporciona un amplio campo visual para la exposición de la colección de arte del dueño. El espacio añadido alberga una moderna cocina en paralelo llena de luz con aperturas a la nueva y espaciosa zona de comedor y acceso al jardín. Un plano limpio y varios elementos de diseño –como una puerta pivotante acristalada que llega del suelo al techo y una balaustrada de cristal en la zona alta de la planta baja– establecen conexión visual entre los distintos espacios así como entre el interior y el exterior.

The renovation takes advantage of the generous spaces, stripping back unnecessary detailing to create spacious rooms, whilst the expansion makes the most of the removal of a conservatory building at the rear of the property, creating a sense of space.

La renovación se beneficia de los grandes espacios, quitando remates innecesarios para conseguir habitaciones espaciosas. Al mismo tiempo, la ampliación se aprovecha de la eliminación de un porche cerrado en la parte de atrás del terreno creando una sensación de espacio.

The rear façade has been carefully remodelled and punctuated with a circular window on the upper floor in reference to the pure geometric forms in the works of renowned British artists Barbara Hepworth and Ben Nicholson.

La cuidada remodelación de la fachada trasera se ha acentuado con una ventana circular en el piso superior. Una referencia a las formas geométricas puras de los trabajos de los reconocidos artistas británicos Barbara Hepworth y Ben Nicholson.

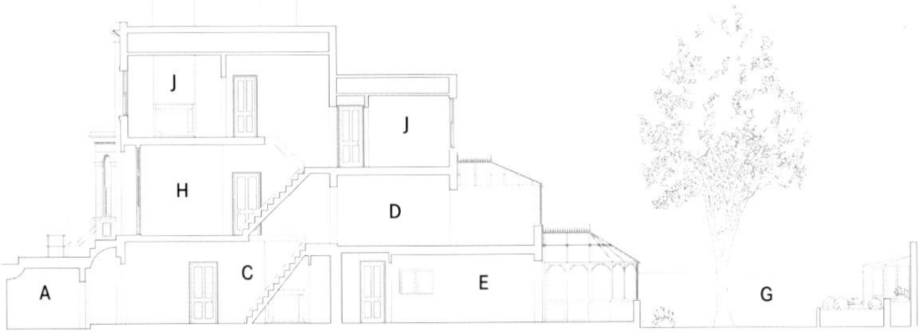

Original section

0 10 m

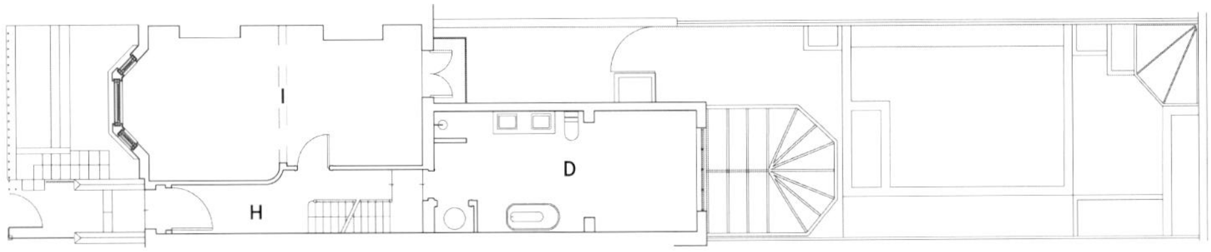

Original ground floor plan

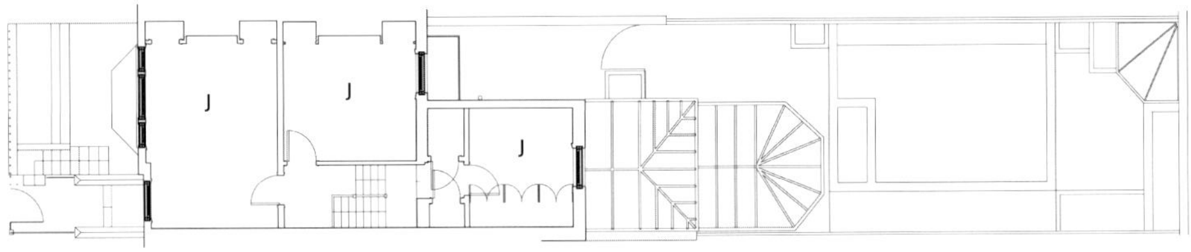

Original first floor plan

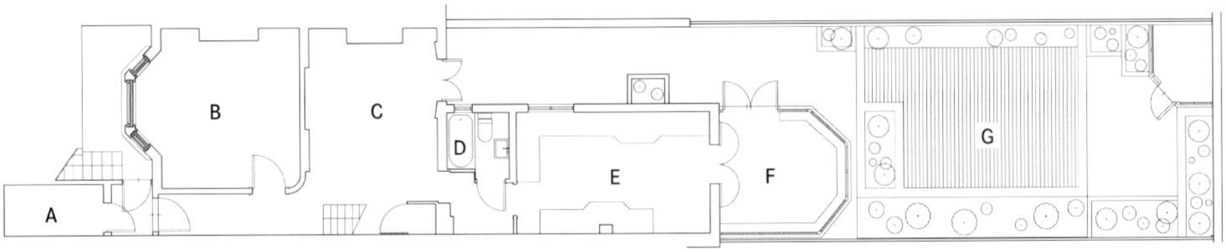

Original lower ground floor plan

0 10 m

A. Bike storage
B. Guest bedroom
C. Playroom
D. Bathroom
E. Kitchen
F. Dining room
G. Terrace
H. Entrance hall
I. Living room
J. Bedroom

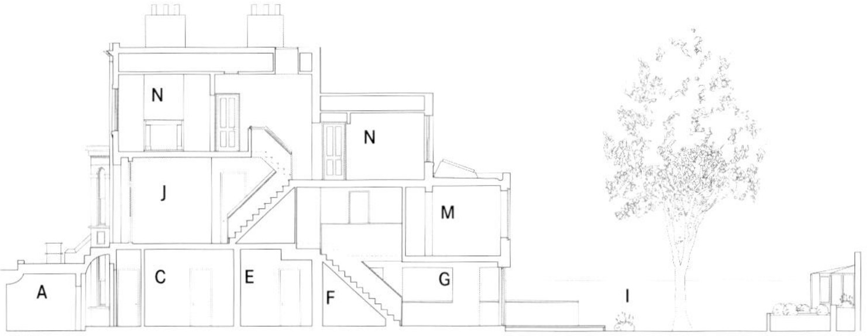

New section

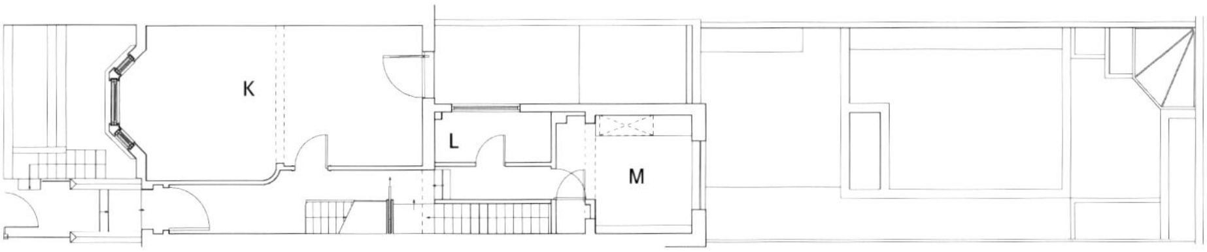

New ground floor plan

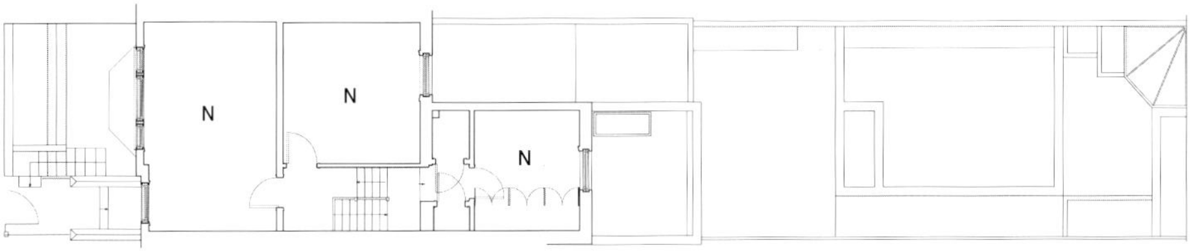

New floor plan

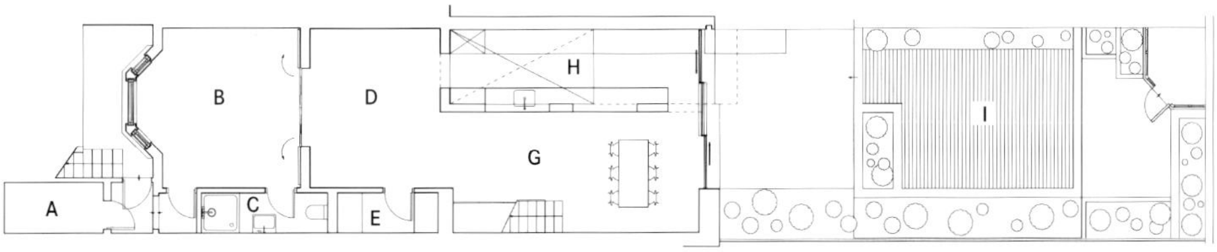

New lower ground floor plan

A. Bike storage
B. Guest bedroom
C. En suite
D. Playroom
E. Utility room
F. Storage
G. Dining room
H. Kitchen
I. Terrace
J. Entrance hall
K. Living room
L. Storage room
M. Bathroom
N. Bedroom

Clean lines are a predominant feature throughout the property. All faux stucco period elements have been stripped out, creating a minimalist backdrop for the display of mid-century furniture classics and a collection of contemporary art.

La característica principal en toda la propiedad son las líneas puras. Se eliminaron los elementos de estuco, creando un telón minimalista para la muestra de muebles de mediados de siglo y una colección de arte contemporáneo.

The window is a central feature of the master bathroom. It provides expansive views of the lushly planted garden from the elegant freestanding claw foot bathtub.

La ventana del baño principal atrae todas las miradas. Desde la elegante bañera exenta con patas se disfruta de amplias vistas sobre la frondosa vegetación del jardín.

THE MEDIC'S HOUSE

A hidden gem nestled in the ordinary

AR Design Studio

LONDON, UNITED KINGDOM

Photos © Martin Gardner

Total Building Area: 2260 sq ft – 210 m^2
Extension Area: 590 sq ft – 55 m^2 // 26% of total area

A growing family's need for additional space meant that their 1950's three-bedroom house had to be extended. The brief called for a large open-plan family space with light, views and access to a garden, as well as two additional bedrooms on the upper floor. The result is a large charcoal grey box at ground level with a full height glazed opening elevation facing the garden. A timber-clad sleeping pod at the first floor level is interlocked with the new volume below.

La necesidad de espacio adicional por parte de una familia que ha ido creciendo, daba lugar a que tuviera que ampliarse su casa de tres dormitorios de la década de los años cincuenta. La idea sugería un gran espacio familiar y abierto con luz, vistas y acceso a un jardín así como dos dormitorios adicionales en la planta superior. El resultado es una gran caja gris de pizarra a nivel del suelo con una altura acristalada que se abre mirando al jardín. Una caja revestida de madera que alberga los dormitorios está conectada con el nuevo volumen de la planta baja.

The overall composition was influenced by the ancient Greek theory of the "Golden Section" in order to provide a well-balanced and proportioned rear elevation.

Para conseguir un alzado trasero proporcionado y equilibrado, se siguió la antigua teoría griega de la proporción áurea en la composición global del proyecto.

The structure is hidden in strategically placed fins that suggest living zones within the open-plan space. Upstairs, the western red cedar addition allows for a lightweight structure that reduces the need for unsightly columns below.

La estructura se esconde en aleros verticales colocados estratégicamente sugiriendo que las zonas comunes conviven con el espacio abierto. En la primera planta, la extensión en madera de cedro canadiense permite una estructura ligera que reduce la necesidad de colocar antiestéticas columnas en la planta baja.

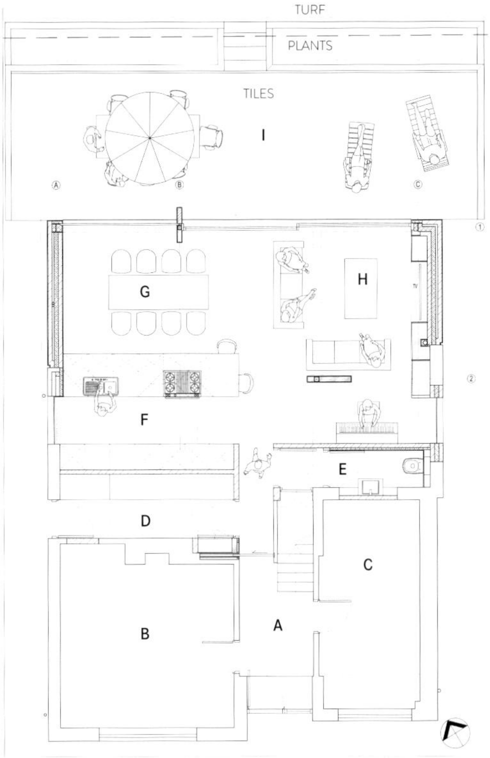

New ground floor plan

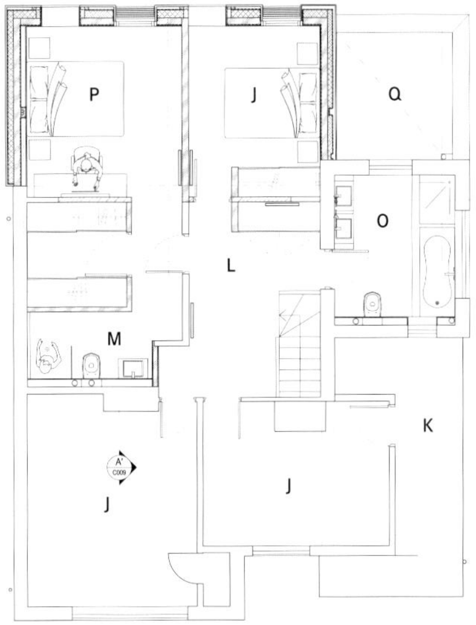

New first floor level

A. Entrance hall
B. Lounge
C. Study
D. Utility room
E. Powder room
F. Kitchen
G. Dining area
H. Sitting area
I. Patio
J. Bedroom
K. Eaves storage
L. Landing
M. En suite bathroom
N. Walk-in-closet
O. Bathroom
P. Master bedroom
Q. Roof

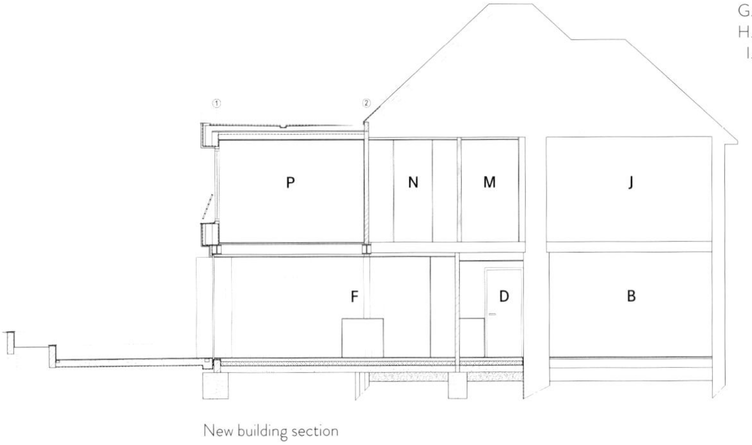

New building section

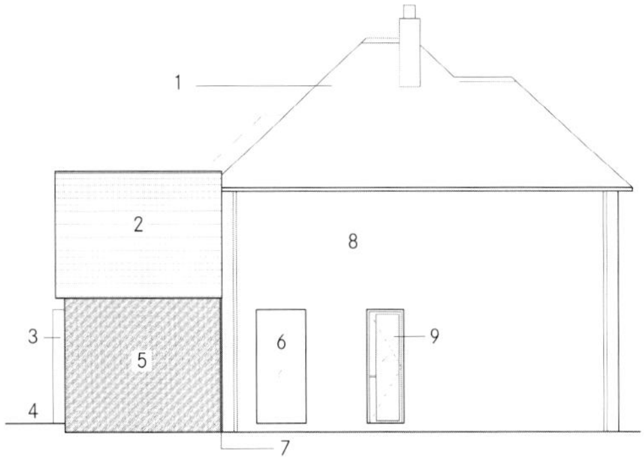

New west elevation

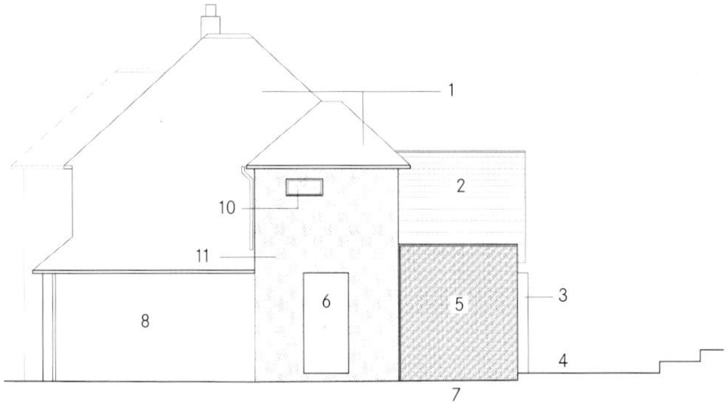

New east elevation

New north elevation

1. Existing roof retained and repaired as existing where necessary
2. Timber cladding
3. White fin
4. Tiled patio
5. Render in grey
6. Frameless glass
7. Shadow gap in dark grey
8. Existing brickwork retained
9. Metal frame glass door, powder coated in grey RAL7016
10. New metal window powder coated in grey
11. White render
12. Metal frame sliding glass doors, powder coated in grey RAL7016
13. Metal frame fixed glass pane, powder coated in grey RAL7016
14. Cables

The flush threshold and continuous floor surface enhance the connection between the interior and the exterior. Large opaque glass panels to the sides allow filtered light to enter deep into the space.

Se refuerza la conexión entre el interior y el exterior con un suelo continuo y sin desniveles. Los grandes paneles de cristal opaco a los lados permiten que la luz filtrada pueda entrar profundamente en el espacio.

T19 HOUSE

An open and bright annex reorganises a townhouse

Reset architecture

VUGHT, THE NETHERLANDS

Photos © Stijn Poelstra-Stijn Style

Total Building Area: 2314 sq ft – 215 m^2
Extension Area: 215 sq ft – 20 m^2 // 9% of total area

A townhouse dating from 1905 was brought up to date to satisfy the contemporary lifestyle of its occupants. The initiative for the renovation of this historic house started with the wish of the client to have an eat-in kitchen directly connected with the backyard. The addition of a double-height open space at the rear of the existing house leads to the reconfiguration of the interior layout where lower and upper ground floors are interrelated and in direct contact with the backyard. A bold volume made of wood and glass stands out beside the brick house. Sophisticated detailing and a visual connection through the annex create synergy between old and new.

Una casa adosada de 1905 se modernizó para satisfacer el actual estilo de vida de sus ocupantes. La iniciativa de remodelación de esta vivienda histórica comenzó con el deseo del cliente de tener una cocina con *office* conectada directamente con el jardín. Al sumarle en la parte de atrás de la casa un espacio abierto de doble altura, cambió la configuración de toda la vivienda, en la que ahora la planta baja y el semisótano están relacionados y en contacto directo con el jardín. Un volumen audaz de madera y cristal destaca tras la casa de ladrillo. Detalles elegantes y la conexión visual a través del anexo crean una sinergia entre lo nuevo y lo antiguo.

In the former situation, the basement was used as storage. Daylight came in muted because of its low ceiling height and an obscure rear façade.

Antes de la renovación, el sótano se usaba como almacén. La baja altura del techo y la oscura fachada trasera impedían que apenas entrase luz natural.

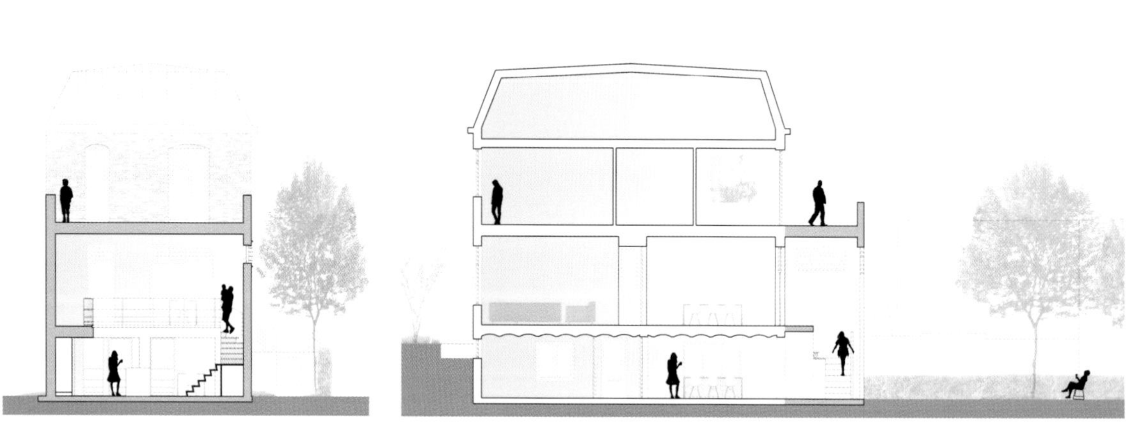

New building sections

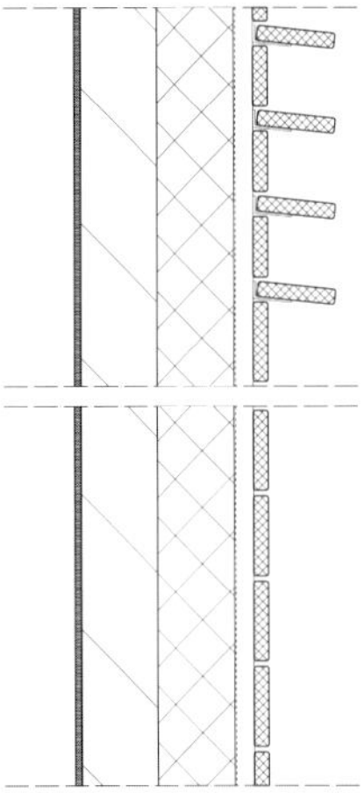

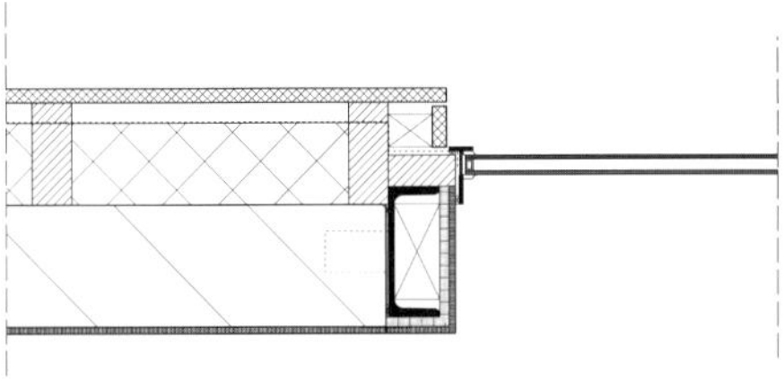

Cladding details

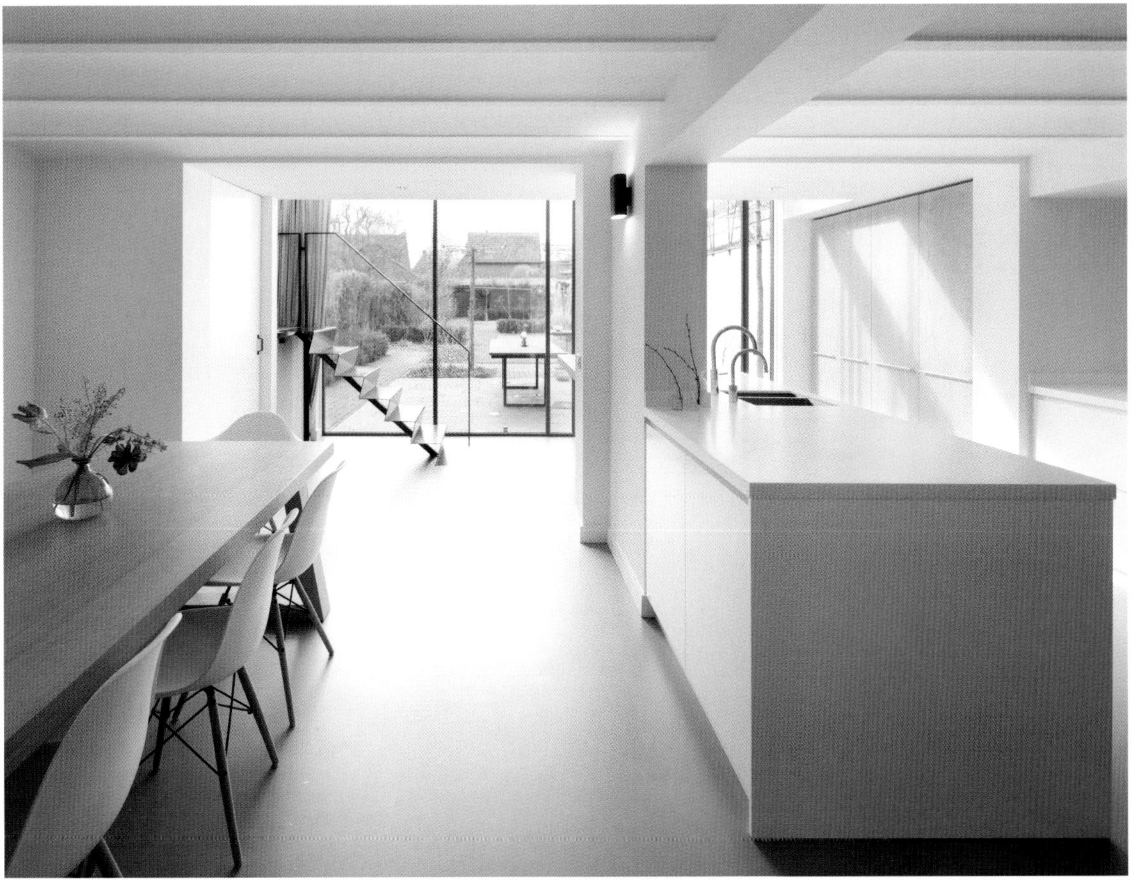

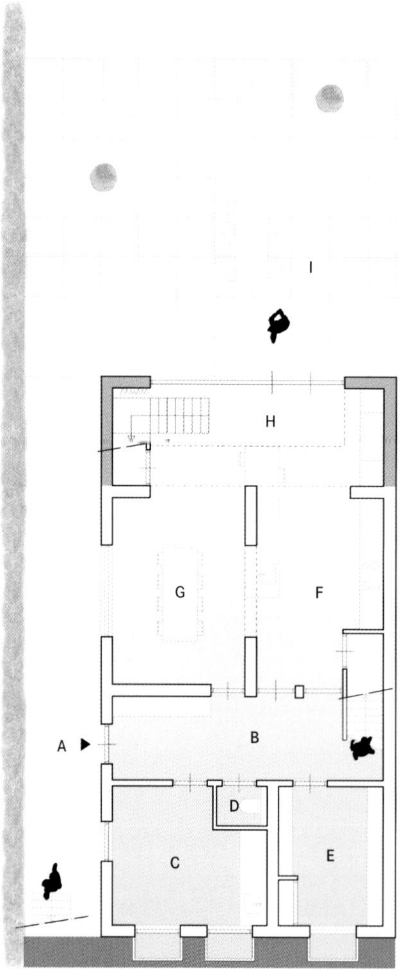

New ground floor plan

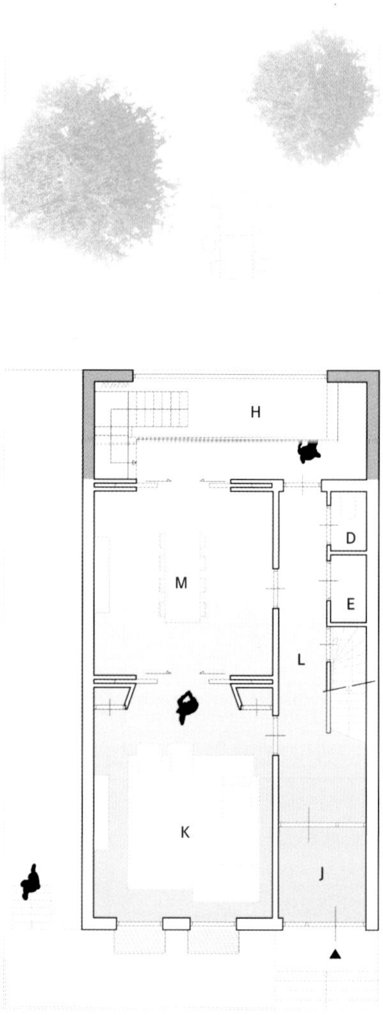

New second floor plan

A. Entrance
B. Service entrance
C. Laundry room
D. WC room
E. Storage room
F. Kitchen
G. Dining room
H. Annex
I. Garden
J. Hall
K. Living room
L. Hallway
M. Dining room

The use of black steel in the interior and exterior enhances the historic character of the house. Detailing and colour scheme are contemporary, avoiding rivalry with the existing classical mouldings on doors, walls and ceilings.

El uso de acero negro en el interior y exterior realza el carácter histórico de la vivienda. Los remates y la paleta de colores que se han utilizado son contemporáneos, evitando rivalizar con los acabados clásicos presentes en puertas, paredes y techos.

Inside, the combination of white walls, warm grey flooring and oak cabinets provides an intimate atmosphere, which naturally adds to the existing historic townhouse. The staircase in the double height space is a sculptural element made of folded steel sheet.

Dentro, la combinación de paredes blancas, suelo de color gris cálido y armarios de roble proporciona una atmósfera íntima que se integra naturalmente con el adosado histórico existente. La escalera en el espacio a doble altura es un elemento arquitectónico hecho de láminas de acero doblado.

POWER HOUSE

A new floor from nowhere

Paul Archer design

LONDON, UNITED KINGDOM

Photos © Andy Stagg

Total Building Area: 2422 sq ft – 225 m^2
Extension Area: 872 sq ft – 81 m^2 // 36% of total area

A typical Victorian terraced house takes a new direction with a highly sculptural timber clad rear extension. The scheme was inspired by the clients' love of the outdoors and a taste for Nordic design. A whole new lower ground floor level has been created beneath the original house. This has an open plan where a variety of activities—cooking, dining, and relaxing—can all take place simultaneously in a flexible arrangement for a growing family. Fully glazed folding doors give direct access to the garden deck.

Una escultural extensión trasera con revestimiento de madera da un nuevo rumbo a una típica casa pareada de estilo victoriano. Al cliente le gustan los espacios exteriores y el diseño nórdico y estas dos características inspiraron el proyecto. Se creó una planta en semisótano por debajo de la casa original. Una zona abierta ideada para una familia en crecimiento que permite realizar toda una serie de actividades –cocinar, comer y relajarse– de forma simultánea. Las puertas correderas acristaladas dan acceso directo al patio y al jardín.

ARSENAL
FOOTBALL

This typical London Victorian terraced house offers a glimpse of the past, lending character, while at the same time adapting to current needs. The new design encompasses a new lower ground floor underneath the original house that has become a focal area for various activities such as cooking, dining and entertaining.

Esta típica casa pareada londinense de estilo victoriano ofrece un destello del pasado, lleno de carácter, al mismo tiempo que se adapta a las necesidades actuales. Este nuevo diseño incluye una nueva planta en semisótano que es el punto central para distintas actividades como cocinar, comer o socializar.

The focal point of the new house is a spacious double-height kitchen and dining area at the rear of the property, which is created by the interplay of interlocking volumes made of frameless glass panels and linear timber panels.

El punto central de la nueva casa es la zona espaciosa y de doble altura donde se encuentran la cocina y el comedor, en la parte de atrás de la vivienda, que se crea por la interacción de volúmenes conectados hechos de paneles de cristal sin marcos y paneles lineales de madera.

A. Patio
B. BBQ area
C. Living area
D. Dining area
E. Breakfast bar
F. Kitchen
G. Utility room
H. Pantry
I. Powder room
J. Play/TV area
K. Storage
L. Entry hall
M. Front reception
N. Rear reception
O. Bedroom
P. Bathroom
Q. Terrace
R. Master bedroom
S. En suite

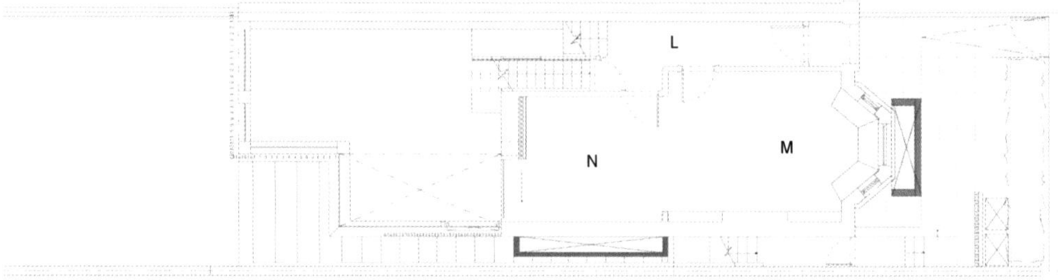

New ground floor plan

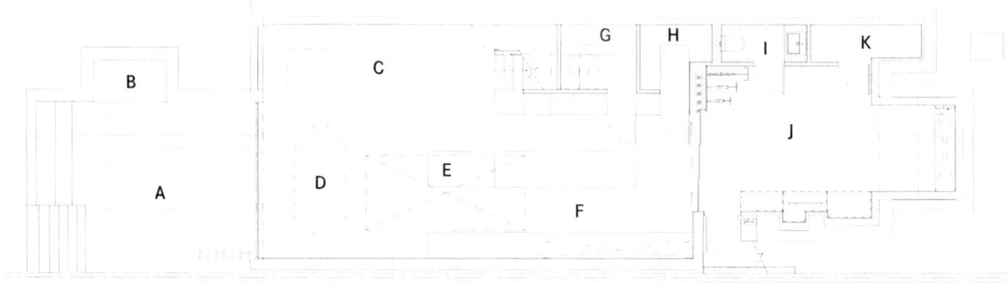

New lower ground floor plan

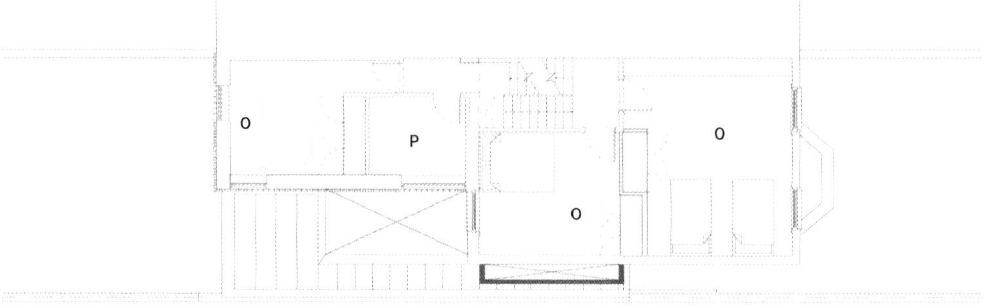

New first floor plan

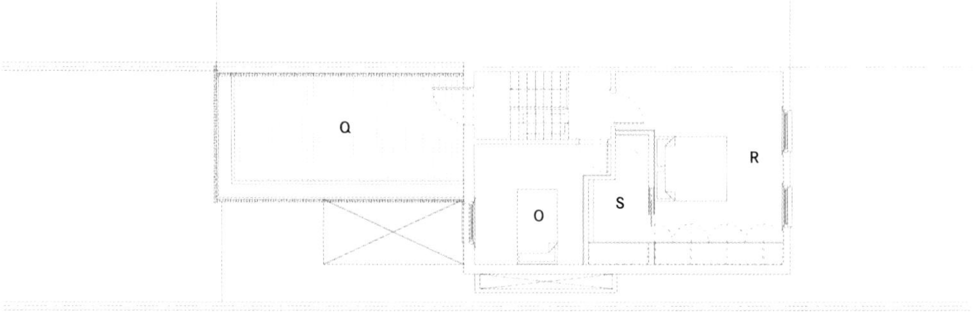

New second floor plan

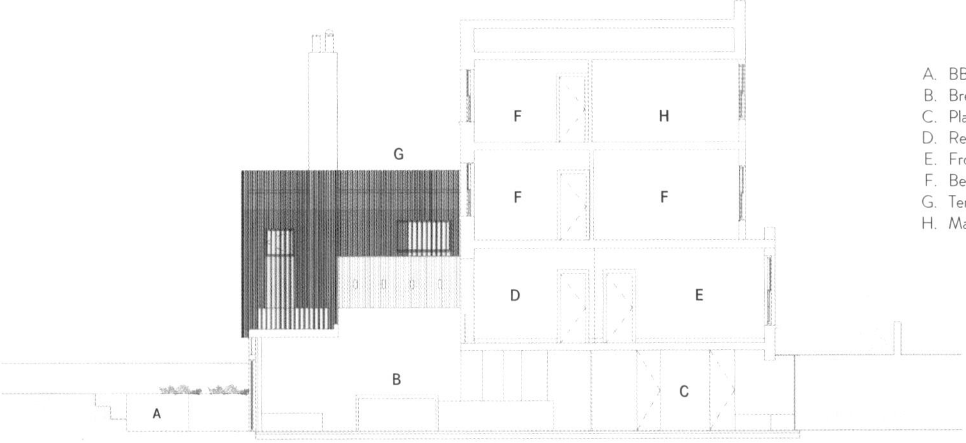

A. BBQ area
B. Breakfast bar
C. Play/TV area
D. Rear reception
E. Front reception
F. Bedroom
G. Terrace
H. Master bedroom

New building section

Wood is put to striking effect and is abundant in all aspects of the scheme from the signature linear cladding, external decking, interior floors, storage spaces disguised as walls and bench seating, and as a kitchen island with breakfast bar.

La madera produce un efecto llamativo y abunda en todos los aspectos del programa, desde el revestimiento lineal distintivo, pasando por el entarimado exterior, los suelos de la vivienda, espacios de almacenamiento ocultos en las paredes y el banco, hasta la isla de cocina con barra de desayuno.

Power House

The upper floors of the extension are clad with a skin of Douglas fir battens, which run both inside and out as exterior cladding and interior wall lining, emphasising the interplay between volumes.

Los pisos superiores de la extensión están revestidos de una piel de listones de pino de Oregón, que se extiende tanto en el interior, forrando las paredes, como en el exterior, revistiendo los muros, enfatizando la interrelación entre los volúmenes.

C2A

An integration of eras

LABorstudio

CHIHUAHUA CITY, MEXICO

Photos © Rafael Gamo

Total Building Area: 3229 sq ft – 300 m²
Extension Area: 2368 sq ft – 220 m² // 73.5% of total area

The project began with the restoration of an old building with a forty square-meter footprint dating from the early twentieth century. Later, the neighbouring three hundred square-meter property was added to the program, providing space for an extension of the existing old building. This extension was conceived as a series of articulated volumes and a staircase that not only connects the different floor levels of the extension, but also acts as a link between the old and new constructions.

El proyecto empezó con la restauración de un antiguo edificio de cuarenta metros cuadrados de planta de principios del siglo XX. Más adelante, la superficie vecina de trescientos metros cuadrados se añadió al programa, facilitando espacio para una ampliación del edificio existente. Esta extensión se concibió como una serie de volúmenes articulados y una escalera que además de conectar los distintos pisos de la ampliación, también es el nexo de unión entre las construcciones antigua y nueva.

The project was originated by a two-storey building in a deteriorated urban environment. This led to a study around the refurbishment of derelict building structures and the exploration of the possibilities of urban regeneration.

El proyecto lo originó un edificio de dos plantas en un entorno urbano deteriorado. Esto llevó a un estudio sobre la remodelación de unas estructuras en ruinas y la exploración de posibilidades de regeneración urbana.

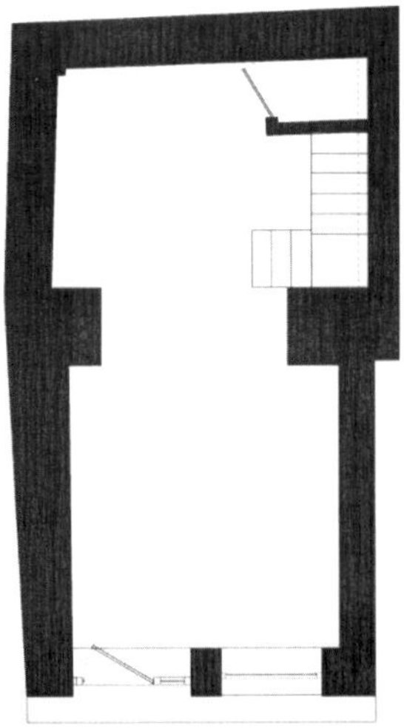

Original ground floor plan

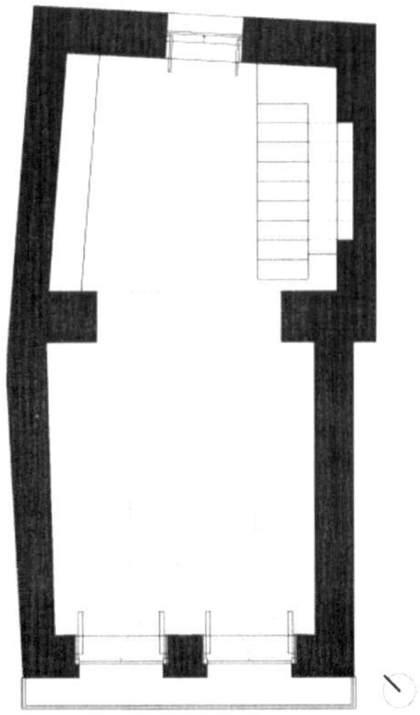

Original second floor plan

New second floor plan

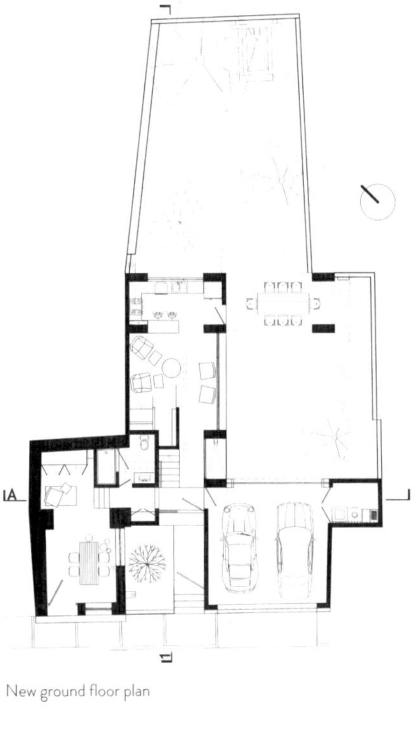

New ground floor plan

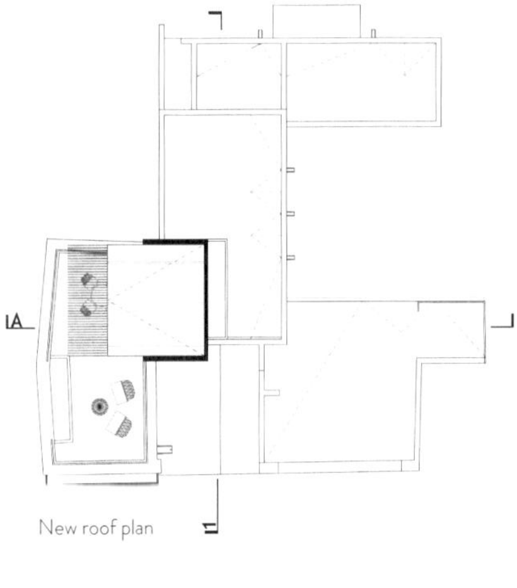

New roof plan

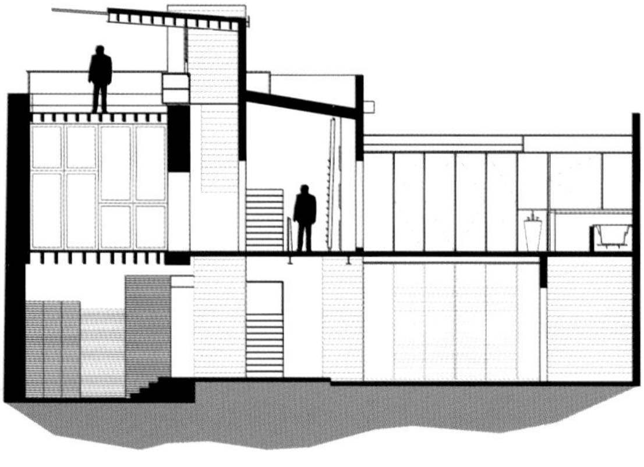

New section A

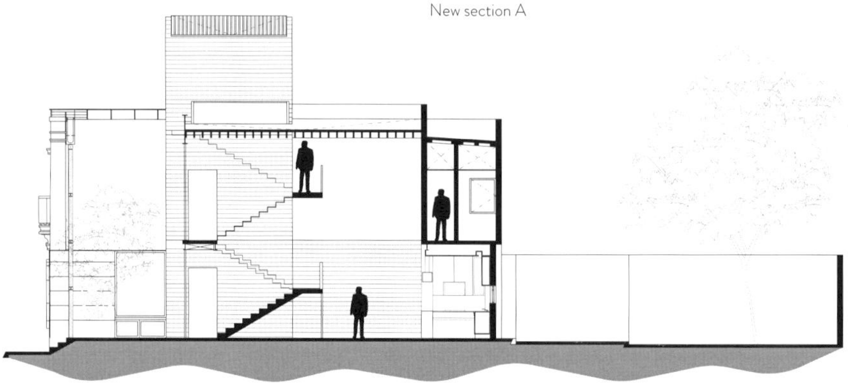

New section 1

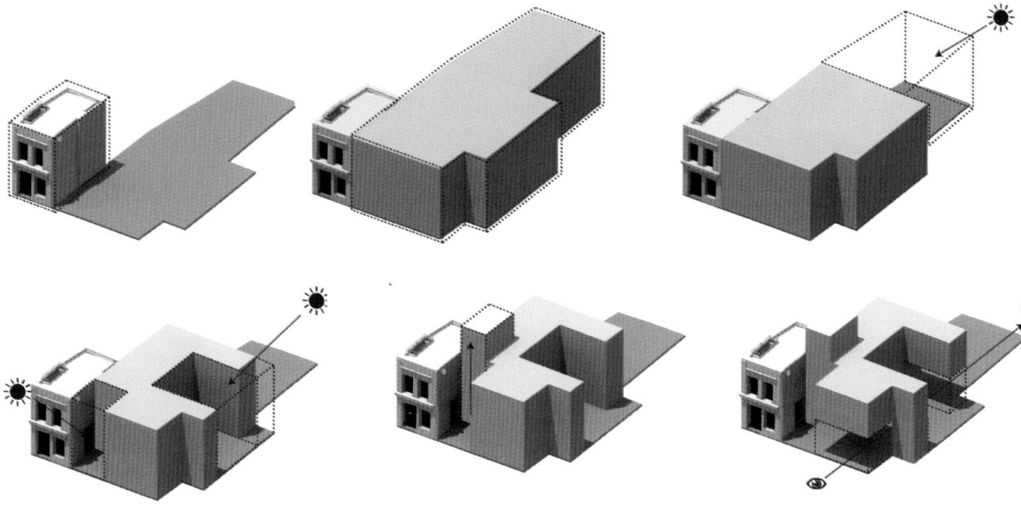

Massing diagrams

All living spaces are interconnected to enhance visual continuity and open to the outdoors wherever possible to maximise a sense of space.

La continuidad visual se refuerza con la conexión de todos los espacios de día. Para maximizar la sensación de espacio, estas estancias se abren al exterior en la medida de sus posibilidades.

The staircase acts as a connector between the existing building and the new extension, whilst creating visual links and long sightlines.

La escalera no solo es el vínculo entre el edificio original y la ampliación, sino que también genera lazos visuales y facilita las vistas dentro del interior de la casa.

CAMPDEN GROVE

Kensington Townhouse

Tigg + Coll architects

LONDON, UNITED KINGDOM

Photos © Andy Matthews

Total Building Area: 3233 sq ft – 300 m^2
Extension Area: 861 sq ft – 80 m^2 // 27% of total area

A traditional and slightly tired townhouse was brought back to life with a sensible renovation and contemporary expansion to reflect the needs of the client's young family, whilst maintaining the classical character of the building. The client wanted to add space with a basement and closet wing extension to create an additional bedroom, a gym, and cinema room. Not only did this provide an opportunity to restructure the property and create larger interconnected spaces, but also to open the interior to a compact garden and give a much greater sense of space.

Una casa adosada tradicional y ligeramente destartalada volvió a brillar con una renovación apropiada y una ampliación contemporánea que refleja las necesidades de la joven familia del cliente, a la vez que mantiene el carácter clásico del edificio. El cliente quería aumentar espacio con un sótano y una extensión en la parte de atrás de la casa para crear un dormitorio adicional, un gimnasio y una sala de cine. Además de proporcionar una oportunidad para reestructurar la propiedad y crear espacios interconectados más amplios, este cambio también permitió abrir el interior a un pequeño jardín y dar mayor sensación de espacio.

The original home was already substantial, but the split levels between a closet wing and main house, and the lack of light to the lower ground floor meant that it felt constrained and dingy.

La vivienda original ya era amplia, pero parecía constreñida y lóbrega, por la diferencia de nivel entre la extensión trasera y la casa principal y la falta de luz en el semisótano.

The basement, lower and upper ground floors are open to a small terraced garden at the back of the property. This was achieved by installing six-meter-tall glazed sliding doors to a double-height void between the lower and raised ground floors.

El sótano, el semisótano y la planta baja están abiertos a un pequeño jardín en terrazas en la parte de atrás de la propiedad. Se consiguió instalando una puerta deslizante de cristal de seis metros de alto en un vacío a doble altura, entre el semisótano y la planta principal.

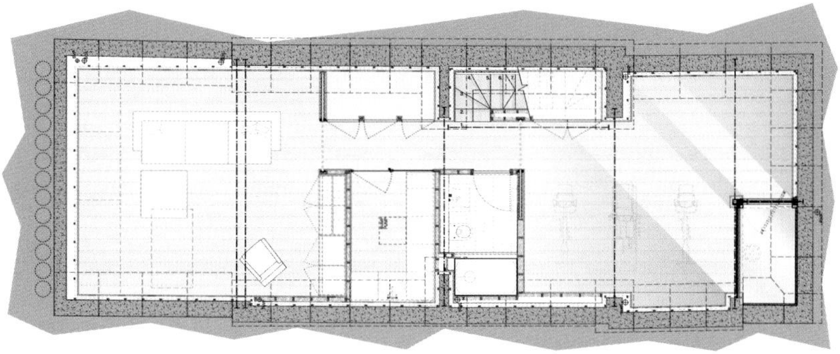

New basement floor plan

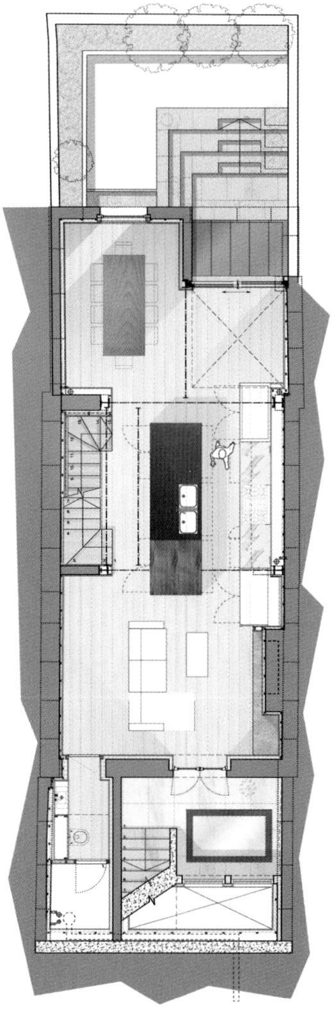

New lower ground floor plan

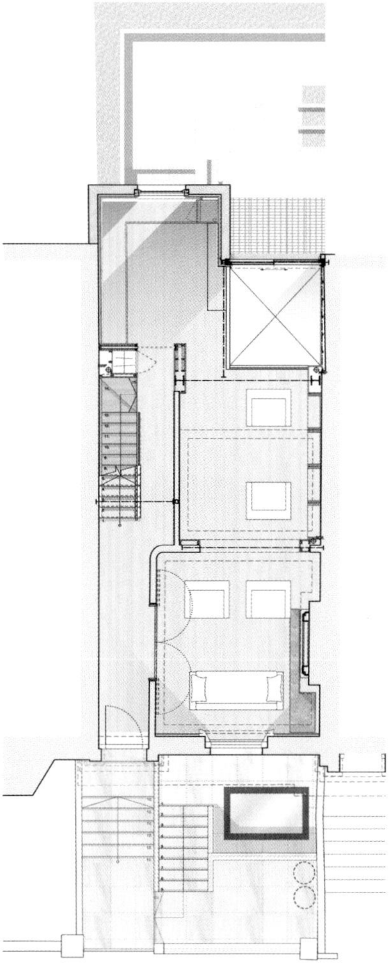

New ground floor plan

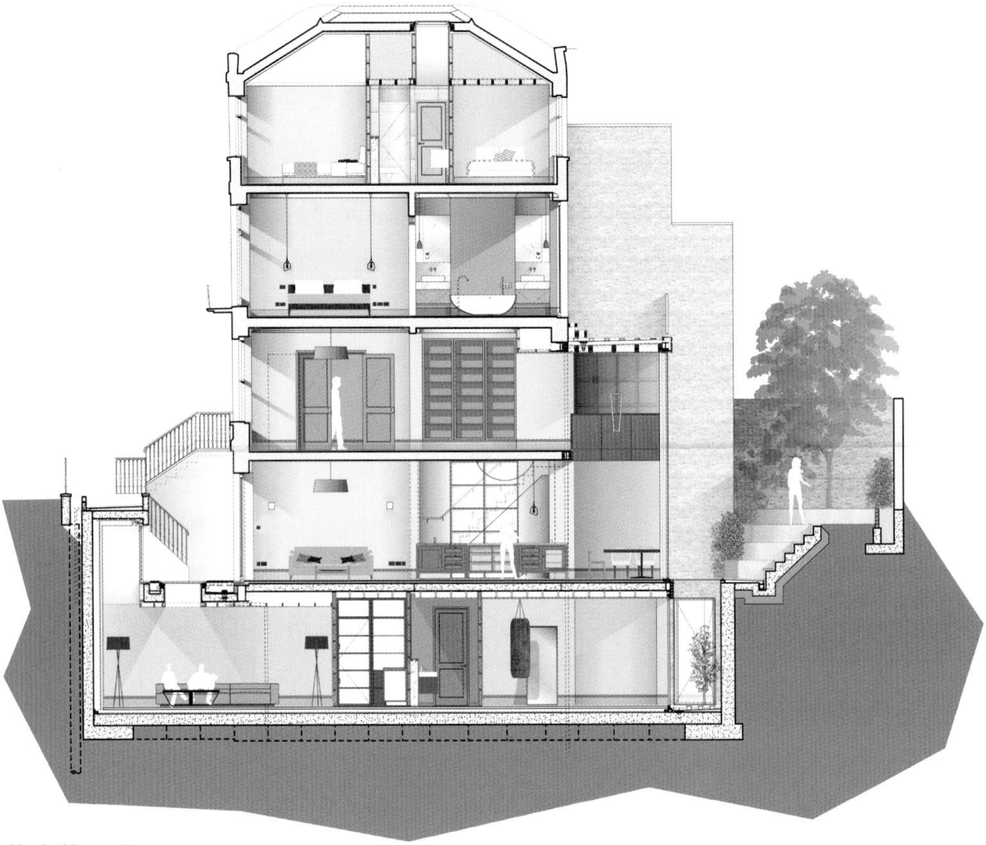

New building section

The basement excavation helped maximize the floor-to-ceiling height and natural light. This turned what had been a dark an unwelcoming series of small rooms into a bright and inviting open-plan kitchen, dining and family room.

La excavación en el sótano ayudó a maximizar la altura de suelo a techo y la luz natural. Esto convirtió lo que habían sido una serie de habitaciones poco atractivas en un espacio abierto luminoso y acogedor que incluía la cocina, el comedor y la zona de estar.

Campden Grove

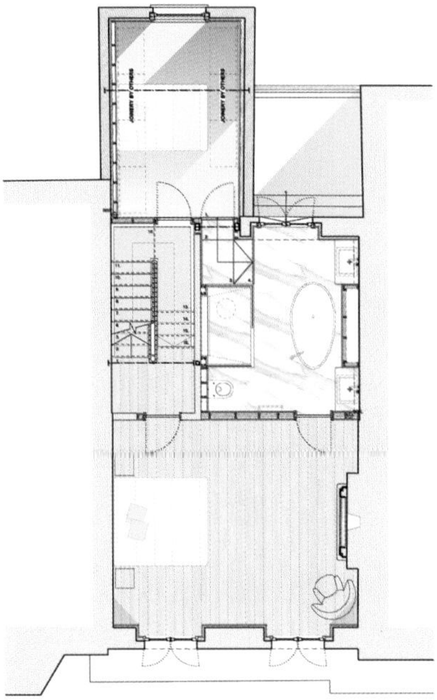
New first floor plan

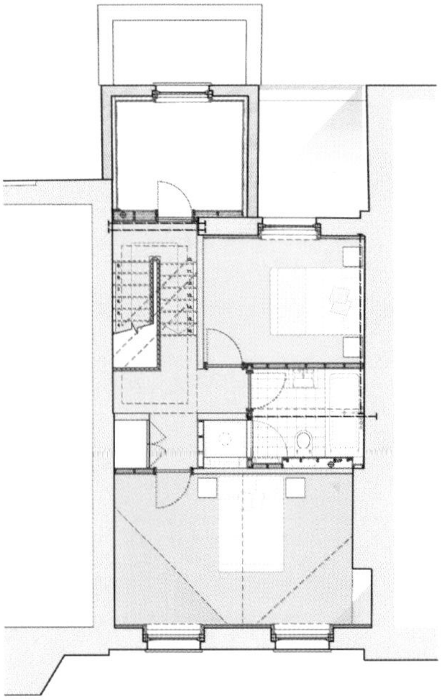
New second floor plan

The client was keen to maintain the traditional character of the property across the upper three storeys, so a more restrained and classical approach was adopted for these.

El cliente deseaba mantener el carácter tradicional de la vivienda en las tres plantas superiores, por lo que en estas se adaptó un enfoque más clásico y contenido.

TRINITY HALL

Subterranean spatial solution

Riach architects

OXFORD, UNITED KINGDOM

Photos © Darrell Godliman

Total Building Area: 4230 sq ft – 393 m²
Extension Area: 1130 sq ft – 105 m² // 27% of total area

This five-storey Victorian house originally belonged to Oxford University. Whilst its interior was subdivided into student flats, the building's original character remained intact. Still, much work needed to be done to adapt its interior to modern living. The existing building didn't have a proper cooking area, so a well-fitted kitchen was tailored to the lifestyle of the family, opened to the rear patio and to the garden beyond. In response to the need to bring more light into the house, a new skylight was placed above the main stairwell and another above the new family room and kitchen.

Esta casa victoriana de cinco plantas pertenecía originariamente a la Universidad de Oxford. Mientras que su interior fue subdividido en pisos de estudiantes, el carácter original del edificio se mantuvo intacto. Aún así, la adaptación del interior a los tiempos actuales exigió mucho trabajo. El edificio original no tenía una zona de cocina apropiada, por lo que se diseñó una cocina bien equipada adecuada al estilo de vida de la familia, que se abre al patio trasero y al jardín. La casa necesitaba más luz, por ello se diseñó una claraboya sobre la escalera principal y otra sobre la zona de estar y la cocina.

The building stands gracefully, boasting its original character. With high ceilings and nice proportions, the architectural essence remained intact, but the excessively compartmentalized interior needed an extensive refurbishment to make the place liveable as a single-family dwelling.

El edificio, que conserva todo su carácter original, rezuma elegancia. Su esencia arquitectónica se mantiene, gracias a los techos altos y proporciones armoniosas. Sin embargo, la división excesiva del interior obligaba a efectuar una gran reforma para convertir la casa en el hogar de una familia.

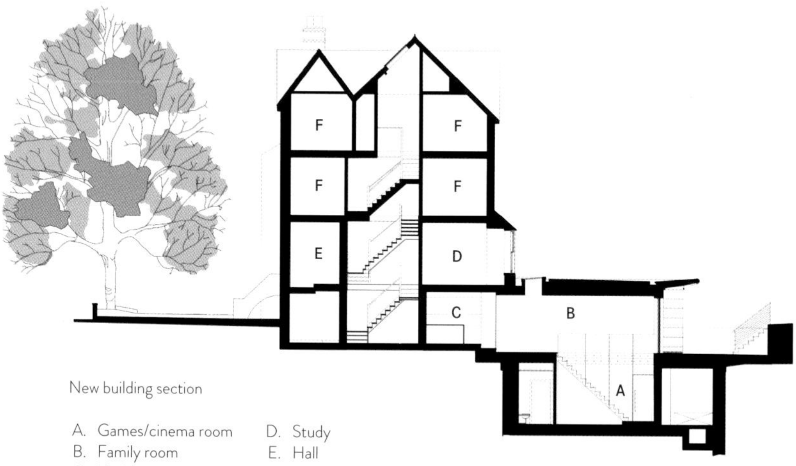

New building section

A. Games/cinema room
B. Family room
C. Kitchen
D. Study
E. Hall
F. Bedroom

The house now extends two floors below ground level: a bright and spacious kitchen and family room now occupy the original basement which was turned into the heart of the home; a new lower basement was designed to accommodate a games room and home cinema.

La vivienda se extiende dos plantas bajo el nivel de calle: una luminosa y espaciosa cocina y una sala de estar ahora ocupan el antiguo sótano, que se ha convertido en el corazón del hogar; se diseñó un nuevo sótano más profundo para albergar una sala de juegos y de cine.

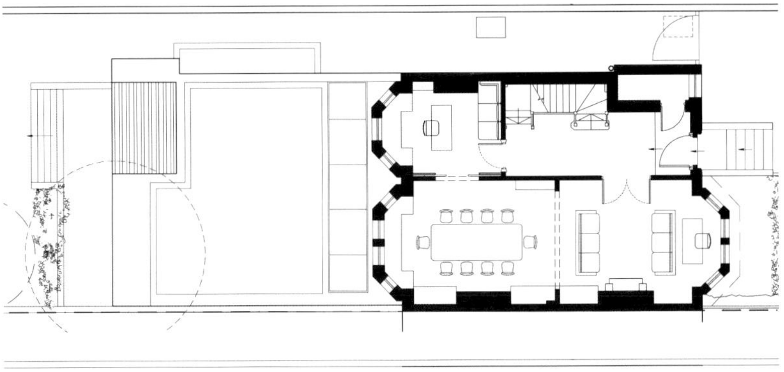

New ground floor plan

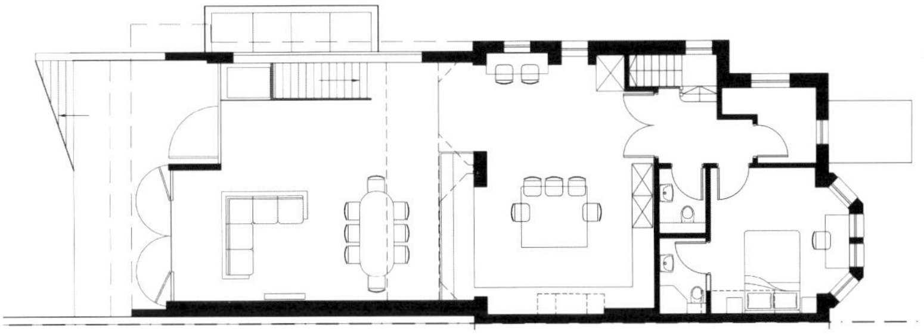

New upper basement floor plan

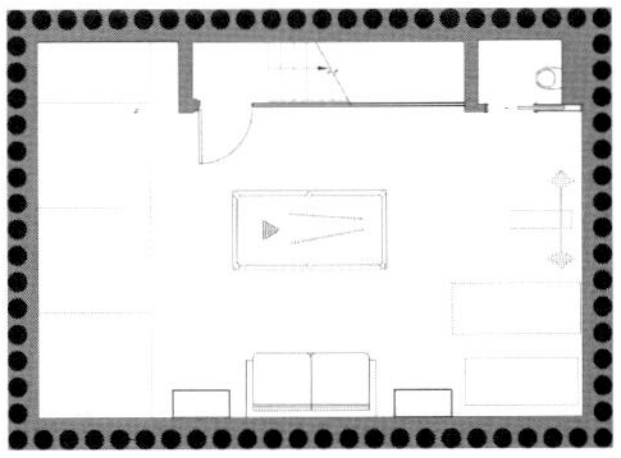

New lower basement floor plan

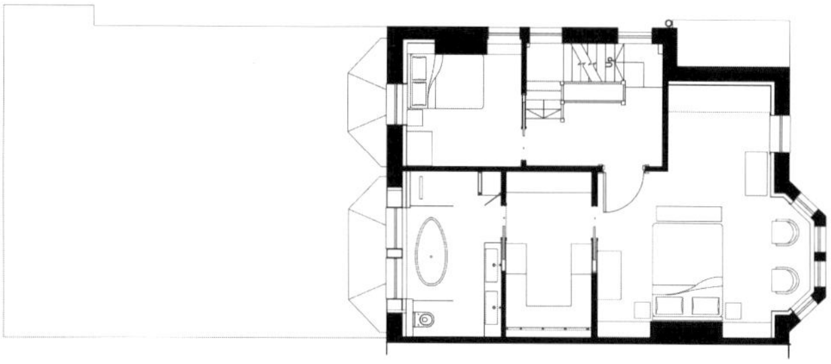

New first floor plan

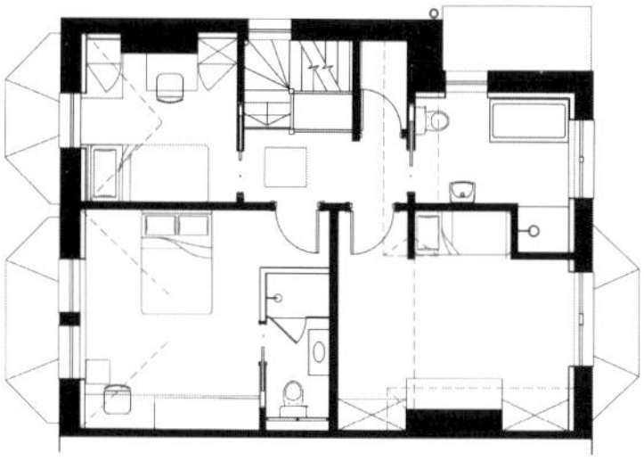

New second floor plan

NE FUME
LE NIL